I0008281

Hands-On Networking with Azure

Build large-scale, real-world apps using Azure networking solutions

Mohamed Waly

BIRMINGHAM - MUMBAI

Hands-On Networking with Azure

Copyright © 2018 Packt Publishing

All rights reserved. No part of this book may be reproduced, stored in a retrieval system, or transmitted in any form or by any means, without the prior written permission of the publisher, except in the case of brief quotations embedded in critical articles or reviews.

Every effort has been made in the preparation of this book to ensure the accuracy of the information presented. However, the information contained in this book is sold without warranty, either express or implied. Neither the author, nor Packt Publishing or its dealers and distributors, will be held liable for any damages caused or alleged to have been caused directly or indirectly by this book.

Packt Publishing has endeavored to provide trademark information about all of the companies and products mentioned in this book by the appropriate use of capitals. However, Packt Publishing cannot guarantee the accuracy of this information.

Commissioning Editor: Vijin Boricha
Acquisition Editor: Rahul Nair
Content Development Editor: Nithin Varghese
Technical Editor: Komal Karne
Copy Editor: Safis Editing
Project Coordinator: Virginia Dias
Proofreader: Safis Editing
Indexer: Mariammal Chettiyar
Graphics: Tom Scaria
Production Coordinator: Arvindkumar Gupta

First published: March 2018

Production reference: 1060318

Published by Packt Publishing Ltd.
Livery Place
35 Livery Street
Birmingham
B3 2PB, UK.

ISBN 978-1-78899-822-2

www.packtpub.com

To the soul of my father, the one I wished to witness such a moment with.

– Mohamed Waly

`mapt.io`

Mapt is an online digital library that gives you full access to over 5,000 books and videos, as well as industry leading tools to help you plan your personal development and advance your career. For more information, please visit our website.

Why subscribe?

- Spend less time learning and more time coding with practical eBooks and Videos from over 4,000 industry professionals

- Improve your learning with Skill Plans built especially for you

- Get a free eBook or video every month

- Mapt is fully searchable

- Copy and paste, print, and bookmark content

PacktPub.com

Did you know that Packt offers eBook versions of every book published, with PDF and ePub files available? You can upgrade to the eBook version at `www.PacktPub.com` and as a print book customer, you are entitled to a discount on the eBook copy. Get in touch with us at `service@packtpub.com` for more details.

At `www.PacktPub.com`, you can also read a collection of free technical articles, sign up for a range of free newsletters, and receive exclusive discounts and offers on Packt books and eBooks.

Contributors

About the author

Mohamed Waly has been interested in IT since he was a student. He has gained many certificates in the IT field. In July 2014, he was recognized as the youngest MVP in the world. He is an author, speaker, and a blogger. He has contributed to the Azure Community in Egypt and open source on Azure. Waly is currently working as an infrastructure consultant for BlueCloud Technologies, designing and implementing solutions for customers across MEA.

This book would not have seen the light without the help of many people. I'd like to thank the team at Packt Publishing—Rahul Nair, Komal Karne, Nithin George, and the other contributors.

I'd like to thank Bert Wolters, Charbel Nemnom, and Sjoukje Zaal for their endless support. Also, my teammates at BlueCloud Technologies—Moataz Shaaban, Karim Hamdy, Mohamed Saeed, Emad Samir, and my manager, Mahmoud Dwidar.

About the reviewers

Charbel Nemnom is a Microsoft Most Valuable Professional (MVP) for cloud and data center management. He has over 17 years of professional experience in the IT field and guides technical teams to optimize the performance of mission-critical enterprise systems.

He has extensive infrastructure expertise and vast knowledge of a variety of Microsoft technologies. He is Microsoft, Cisco, and VMware certified, and holds the following credentials—VCA-DCV, MCP, MCSA, MCTS, MCITP, MCS, MCSE, CCNP, ITIL®, and PMP®. You can follow him on Twitter at @CharbelNemnom.

Bert Wolters is the lead consultant of the hybrid cloud and apps business unit at the Dutch company InSpark.

In 2008, he decided to specialize in Microsoft infrastructure technology, focusing on system and platform management, and is still riding Microsoft's wave of innovation, looking forward to experimenting with every single new feature of Microsoft Azure. Driven by the will to gain and share knowledge, he's involved in the global Experts Live Community Foundation.

He currently advises companies how to get the most out of their Azure platform implementation or System Center Suite.

Sjoukje Zaal is a Microsoft Azure MVP and a principal architect with over 15 years of experience providing architecture, development, consultancy, and design expertise. She works at Ordina as a system integrator, based in the Netherlands.

She is very active in the Microsoft Community as a cofounder of SP&C NL and MixUG, writer, and a public speaker who is on MSDN/TechNet. She is also the author of *Architecting Microsoft Azure Solutions*.

Packt is searching for authors like you

If you're interested in becoming an author for Packt, please visit `authors.packtpub.com` and apply today. We have worked with thousands of developers and tech professionals, just like you, to help them share their insight with the global tech community. You can make a general application, apply for a specific hot topic that we are recruiting an author for, or submit your own idea.

Table of Contents

Preface

Microsoft Azure networking is one of the most valuable and important offerings in Azure. It's impossible to imagine an environment without networks. No matter what solution you are building for the cloud, you'll find a compelling use for Azure networking. This book will get you up-to-speed on Microsoft Azure networking by teaching you how to use the different networking services. Based on real-world scenarios, you will be able to leverage secure design patterns. By reading this book, you will develop a strong networking foundation for Azure Virtual Machines, and for expanding your on-premise environment to Azure.

This book starts with an introduction to Microsoft Azure Networking and how to create Azure Virtual Networks with subnets of different types within them. This book will also help you understand the architecture of Azure networks and how it integrates with other Azure services. You will then learn the best practices for designing your Azure VM networks, whether Windows or Linux-based. You will also learn how to expand your networks into Azure, and how to use Azure DNS. Moreover, you will master best practices to deal with Azure Load Balancers (followed by the role of Azure Traffic Manager) and the solutions they offer in different scenarios. Finally, this book demonstrates the workings of Azure Application Gateway, which offers various layer-7 load balancing capabilities for applications.

Who this book is for

This book targets developers, IT professionals, and even database admins who have experience of working with Microsoft Azure and want to make the most of Azure networking services. It would also be a great guide for network engineers who would like to learn Azure.

What this book covers

Chapter 1, *Azure Virtual Networks 101*, introduces Azure and its models in addition to Azure Virtual Networks and subnets, and how to create and manage them. By the end of the chapter, you will have learned how to automate manual tasks implemented throughout the chapter using Azure PowerShell and Azure CLI 2.0.

Chapter 2, *Delving into Azure Virtual Networks*, introduces Azure networking architecture and what is going on behind the scenes. Also, you will learn how to work with Virtual Networks service endpoints and network security groups. By the end of the chapter, you will have learned how to automate manual tasks.

Chapter 3, *Azure Network for VMs*, introduces Azure VMs and how to design and implement networking solutions for Azure VMs. By the end of the chapter, you will have learned how to automate manual tasks.

Chapter 4, *Network Connectivity Scenarios in Azure*, introduces the most common scenarios for extending your on-premises to Azure, which includes how to implement those scenarios.

Chapter 5, *Azure DNS*, introduces how to use Azure DNS as a service, managing your zones on Azure, delegating zones, and even working with reverse DNS zones in Azure. By the end of the chapter, you will have learned how to automate manual tasks.

Chapter 6, *Azure Load Balancers*, introduces Azure Load Balancer and its importance, followed by a step-by-step guide on how to configure Azure Load Balancer.

Chapter 7, *Azure Traffic Manager*, introduces Azure Traffic Manager and its importance, followed by a step-by-step guide on how to configure Azure Traffic Manager. By the end of the chapter, you will have learned how to automate manual tasks.

Chapter 8, *Azure Application Gateway*, introduces Azure Application Gateway and its importance, followed by a step-by-step guide on how to configure Azure Application Gateway.

To get the most out of this book

It's highly recommended to have knowledge of virtualization and networking, such as Hyper-V/VMware/Citrix, or CCNA .

Having knowledge of other Azure services will be a great benefit. You can check out my other book about Azure Storage at the following link: https://www.packtpub.com/big-data-and-business-intelligence/learning-microsoft-azure-storage.

Download the color images

We also provide a PDF file that has color images of the screenshots/diagrams used in this book. You can download it here: https://www.packtpub.com/sites/default/files/downloads/HandsOnNetworkingwithAzure_ColorImages.pdf.

Conventions used

There are a number of text conventions used throughout this book.

`CodeInText`: Indicates code words in text, database table names, folder names, filenames, file extensions, pathnames, dummy URLs, user input, and Twitter handles. Here is an example: "Navigate to Azure portal, and search for `network security groups`."

Any command-line input or output is written as follows:

```
$NSubnet = New-AzureRMVirtualNetworkSubnetConfig -Name NSubnet -
AddressPrefix 192.168.1.0/24
$GWSubnet = New-AzureRMVirtualNetworkSubnetConfig -Name GatewaySubnet -
AddressPrefix 192.168.2.0/27
```

Bold: Indicates a new term, an important word, or words that you see onscreen. For example, words in menus or dialog boxes appear in the text like this. Here is an example: "Once you have clicked on **Create**, the NSG will be created within seconds."

Warnings or important notes appear like this.

Tips and tricks appear like this.

Get in touch

Feedback from our readers is always welcome.

General feedback: Email `feedback@packtpub.com` and mention the book title in the subject of your message. If you have questions about any aspect of this book, please email us at `questions@packtpub.com`.

Errata: Although we have taken every care to ensure the accuracy of our content, mistakes do happen. If you have found a mistake in this book, we would be grateful if you would report this to us. Please visit `www.packtpub.com/submit-errata`, selecting your book, clicking on the Errata Submission Form link, and entering the details.

Piracy: If you come across any illegal copies of our works in any form on the Internet, we would be grateful if you would provide us with the location address or website name. Please contact us at `copyright@packtpub.com` with a link to the material.

If you are interested in becoming an author: If there is a topic that you have expertise in and you are interested in either writing or contributing to a book, please visit `authors.packtpub.com`.

Reviews

Please leave a review. Once you have read and used this book, why not leave a review on the site that you purchased it from? Potential readers can then see and use your unbiased opinion to make purchase decisions, we at Packt can understand what you think about our products, and our authors can see your feedback on their book. Thank you!

For more information about Packt, please visit `packtpub.com`.

1
Azure Virtual Networks 101

Introduction

This chapter introduces Azure Virtual Networks, differences between the Azure Service Management and Azure Resource Manager models, and some key points that will help you to design your solution. We will also cover Azure Virtual Network subnet types and in which scenarios these subnets would be used. Finally, you will learn how to automate all the manual tasks that have been implemented throughout the chapter.

Learning outcomes

The following topics will be covered:

- Introduction to Microsoft Azure Networks
- Azure terminologies
- **Azure Service Management (ASM)** versus the **Azure Resource Manager (ARM)** model
- Azure **Virtual Network (VNet)**
- Automating your tasks

Technical requirements

To go through the book smoothly, you need to have the following:

- **An Azure subscription**: You can sign up for a trial from the following link `https://azure.microsoft.com/en-us/free/`
- **PowerShell**: Make sure you have PowerShell V3, by running the following cmdlet to check the version `$PSVersionTable.PSVersion`
- **Azure PowerShell module**: You can download it from the following link `https://www.microsoft.com/web/handlers/webpi.ashx/getinstaller/WindowsAzurePowershellGet.3f.3f.3fnew.appids`
- **Azure CLI 2.0**: You can download it for your OS from the following links:
    - **Windows**: `https://docs.microsoft.com/en-us/cli/azure/install-azure-cli-windows?view=azure-cli-latest`
    - **Linux**: `https://docs.microsoft.com/en-us/cli/azure/install-azure-cli-linux?view=azure-cli-latest`
    - **Mac**: `https://docs.microsoft.com/en-us/cli/azure/install-azure-cli-macos?view=azure-cli-latest`

Introduction to Microsoft Azure Networks

One of the major facts in our life is networking. In the beginning, human beings used to make networks communicate with each other to fulfill their needs. That's why when the computer revolution took place, networks were a very important piece of the puzzle to let computers communicate with each other.

Through the whole of the IT revolution, networks used to be an indispensable part of every IT environment to have a properly functioning environment. It is no surprise that networking is a vital part of cloud from many aspects, starting from the remote connection to your Azure VMs, to spanning your environment across on-premises and Azure. You will notice that networks are used with almost all Azure services, this includes, but is not limited to Azure VMs, Azure SQL Databases, Azure Web Apps, and so on.

At the time of writing, Microsoft Azure is generally available in 36 regions, with plans announced for six additional regions, as shown in the following table:

Region	Status	Location
East US	Generally available	Virginia
East US 2	Generally available	Virginia
Central US	Generally available	Iowa
North Central US	Generally available	Illinois
South Central US	Generally available	Texas
West Central US	Generally available	West Central US
West US	Generally available	California
West US 2	Generally available	West US 2
US Gov Virginia	Generally available	Virginia
US Gov Iowa	Generally available	Iowa
US DoD East	Generally available	Virginia
US DoD Central	Generally available	Iowa
US Gov Arizona	Generally available	Arizona
US Gov Texas	Generally available	Texas
Canada East	Generally available	Quebec City
Canada Central	Generally available	Toronto
Brazil South	Generally available	Sao Paulo State
North Europe	Generally available	Ireland
West Europe	Generally available	Netherlands
UK West	Generally available	Cardiff
UK South	Generally available	London
Germany Central	Generally available	Frankfurt
Germany Northeast	Generally available	Magdeburg
France Central	Coming soon	Paris

France South	Coming soon	Marseille
Southeast Asia	Generally available	Singapore
East Asia	Generally available	Hong Kong
Australia East	Generally available	New South Wales
Australia Southeast	Generally available	Victoria
China East	Generally available	Shanghai
China North	Generally available	Beijing
Central India	Generally available	Pune
West India	Generally available	Mumbai
South India	Generally available	Chennai
Japan East	Generally available	Tokyo, Saitama
Japan West	Generally available	Osaka
Korea Central	Generally available	Seoul
Korea South	Generally available	Busan
Australia Central 1	Coming soon	Canberra
Australia Central 2	Coming soon	Canberra
South Africa West	Coming soon	Cape Town
South Africa North	Coming soon	Johannesburg

This global presence means you can build your networks in the nearest region, and access them from anywhere in the world, considering that Microsoft keeps building new data centers in new regions, so latency between your on-premises environment and Azure is decreased.

You can find out the nearest region to you with the lowest latency via the following website `http://www.azurespeed.com/`. Azure services are available in 140 countries around the globe and support 17 languages, and 24 currencies.

Azure terminologies

Due to an overlap of terms and some misperceptions about the ways that Azure services are delivered, terminology is a sticking point even for people who have been working with the technology for some time. The following table provides accurate, but short definitions for the terms related to Azure services. These definitions will be expanded upon in detail throughout the book, so don't worry if you are confused at first:

Term	Definition
On-premises	Means that your data center is hosted and managed at a location your company manages.
Off-premises	Means that your data center is hosted and managed in a remote place (for example, hosted and managed outside your company).
Azure Virtual Machine	The feature of providing VMs to Azure subscribers.
Blade	The window that pops up when you click on one of the Azure services in the Azure portal, such as virtual machines.
Journey	A set of blades or chain of selections. For instance, when you select VMs inside the Azure portal, click on an existing VM and then select its settings.
Resource group	Provides a logical container for Azure resources (to help manage resources that are often used together).
Virtual network	Allows VMs and services that are part of the same virtual network to access each other. However, services outside the virtual network have no way of connecting to services hosted within virtual networks unless you decide to do so.
Fault domain	A group of resources that could fail at the same time. For example, they are all running on a single rack, sharing the same power source and physical network switch.
Upgrade/update domain	A group of resources that can be updated simultaneously during system upgrades.
Network security group (**NSG**)	Determines the protocols, ports, and who and what can access Azure VMs remotely.

ASM versus ARM model

Previously, Azure used to provide its services via two portals, but recently, Microsoft discontinued the ASM (Classic) portal. However, if you have any services that were running in the classic portal you do not have to worry about them because they have been migrated to Azure ARM portal. Considering that these services would follow the old ASM model. Also, you will note that in the new Azure portal there are two flavors for them. For example, there will be **Virtual Machines**, and **Virtual Machines (Classic)**.

Historically, Azure services were provided via one portal before 2014, the classic portal, which can be accessed via the following link `https://manage.windowsazure.com/`. As of now, this portal will redirect to the ARM portal.

The model that was used for that portal is called the **ASM model**, within which each resource existed independently. You could not manage your resources together, you had to build up and track each resource. For example, you will have to manage the networks from the **NETWORKS** blade, and the same goes for the storage, virtual machines, and so on. So, when your environment gets bigger, there will be chaos in the management scheme. You will have to know which Azure Virtual Machines are using which virtual networks to do its communications, and that might lead to some critical situations, such as reaching the limits of the allowed number of public IPs, and whenever you need to add a new public IP to be used for a VM in your environment, you would not be able to do so because of the poor management of resources. This would not be your only concern while working with the ASM model. If you want to delete a solution with multiple resources, you will have to do it with each resource manually, and so on.

This is how the classic portal looked:

Figure 1.1: Azure Classic portal

Azure portal (ARM model)

In 2014, Microsoft launched a new portal that follows a new model, called the **ARM model**, which can be accessed via the following link `https://portal.azure.com/`.

When you open the Azure portal, it will look as follows:

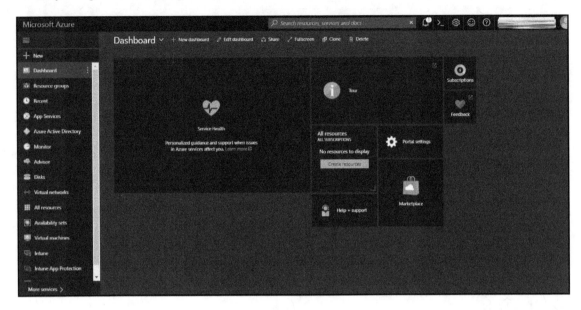

Figure 1.2: Azure portal

This model depends on the concept of resource groups, which means you can group all your resources within a container, resulting in resources being deployed in parallel. As a result, you will not face the same problems as you did with the ASM model.

The following diagram describes the deployed resources through the ARM model:

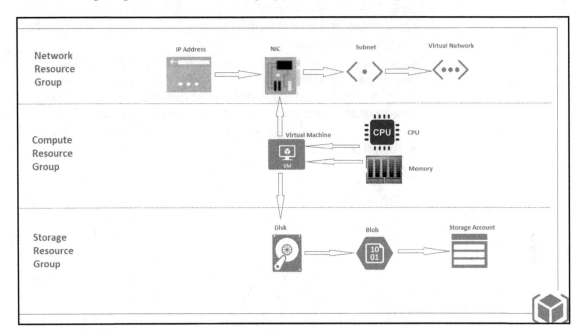

Figure 1.3: Resource manager management model at a high level

Here are the benefits you will gain using that portal:

- Ability to manage your resources as a group instead of managing them separately.
- Using **Role-Based Access Control** (**RBAC**) to control access to resources, so that you can assign permissions to a user on a resource or some resources, but not to other resources (as it was in the classic portal).
- Using tags to organize and classify your resources, which can help you with billing. For example, you might want to monitor the billing of some resources that make up a solution, for example, a web server. By assigning a tag to the resources that make up that solution, you would be able to monitor its billing, and so on.

- Support the usability of JSON to deploy resources instead of using the portal:
    - Deploy resources in parallel instead of deploying them sequentially, and waiting until every resource deployment finishes to deploy another one.
    - Specify dependencies during the resources deployment. For example, a VM will not be created until a storage account and a virtual network get deployed, because the VM VHD would need a place to be stored in and an IP address from a virtual network.
    - Reuse of the JSON template to deploy solutions with the same specifications.

ARM key points

For a better understanding of the ARM model, you might need to consider the following key points:

- Resources with the same lifecycle should be gathered in the same resource group
- Resources in different regions can be in the same resource group
- Every resource must be assigned to a resource group, so whenever you want to move a resource between resource groups you must remove it from its current resource group and then add it to the new resource group
- Resource groups support RBAC, wherein a user can have access to some specific resources, and have no access to the others
- Some resources can be shared across resource groups such as storage accounts
- ARM virtual machines can only be placed in ARM storage accounts
- You cannot create a virtual machine using the ARM model and assign it to a virtual network built using the ASM model
- You cannot use a prebuilt image that was created by ASM APIs to build a VM using the ARM model, but as a workaround you can copy the VHD files from the storage account in the classic portal to a storage account created in the ARM model

- You can migrate assets from the ASM model to the ARM model
- Every resource must be assigned to a resource group, so whenever you want to move a resource between resource groups you must remove it from its current resource group, and then add it to the new resource group

You can change the background of the portal by double-clicking on any unused area of the dashboard. You can navigate between four colors (blue, dark blue, white, and black). For further information about the difference between the ARM and ASM models, check out the following article: `https://blogs.technet.microsoft.com/meamcs/2016/12/22/difference-between-azure-service-manager-and-azure-resource-manager/`.

Azure VNet

As you have a network in your on-premises (private data center) to facilitate the communication between your machines/devices and even to secure and isolate machines/devices from each other, you will need to do the same tasks in the cloud. That is why Microsoft offers Azure VNet.

Azure VNet is one of the most commonly used Microsoft Azure Networking services. Azure VNet is sort of like a LAN within which you can have address spaces that can be divided into multiple subnets. Considering that, only private IPs ranges can be used for the address spaces and their subnets.

The subnets within each address space are automatically routed. The address range of a subnet that is in use cannot be edited.

Azure VNet benefits

Azure VNet has many benefits and capabilities. The following benefits are some of them:

- **Isolation**: Each virtual network is isolated from other virtual networks. Therefore, you can have your dev/test environment in a virtual network separated from the production environment that exits in other virtual networks.
- **Communicating with other VNets**: By default, virtual networks are isolated from each other. However, you can reach out resources in another virtual network, because virtual networks can be connected to each other.
- **Broad network access**: By default, all Azure services have access to the internet, which means you can access Azure services from wherever you want, using whatever you want, as long you have an internet connection.
- **Hybrid connectivity**: Azure VNet can be spanned to your data center. As a result, you will be able to connect to both your Azure resources and on-premises resources privately without the need to connect via the internet.
- **Security**: You can secure your virtual networks by setting rules that determine which inbound and outbound traffic can be flowed to and outside the virtual network.

Creating Azure VNet

Creating an Azure VNet is a pretty straightforward process. To do this task, follow these steps:

1. Open the ARM portal and log in using the account associated with your Azure subscription.

2. Once logged in, navigate to **More services**, and search for `virtual network`, as shown in the following screenshot:

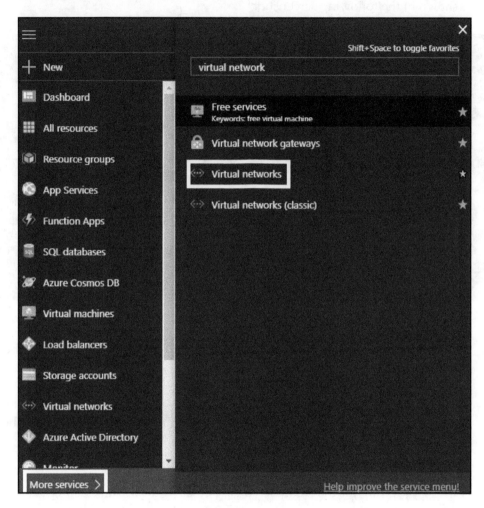

Figure 1.4: Searching for virtual networks blade

3. You will be navigated to a new blade, wherein you can display the virtual networks you have created, and you can also create new virtual networks, as shown in the following screenshot:

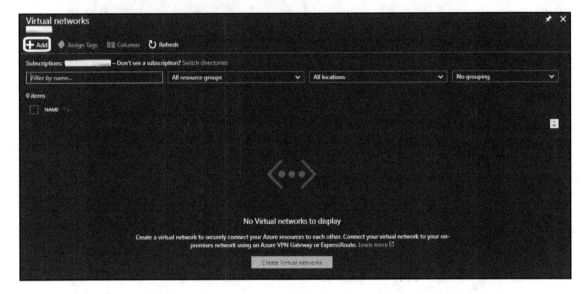

Figure 1.5: Virtual networks blade

4. Click on **Add**, and a new blade will be opened for which you have to fill the following fields:
   - **Name**: The name of the virtual network.
   - **Address space**: The virtual network's address range in CIDR notion.
   - **Subscription**: If you have multiple subscriptions associated to the account you have logged in with, you have to specify which subscription will be charged for this service.
   - **Resource group**: Specify whether you want to create a new resource group for the resource you are creating, or use an existing one.
   - **Location**: The region on which this virtual network will operate.
   - **Subnet-name**: The name of the first subnet in the virtual network you are creating.
   - **Subnet | Address range**: The subnet's address range in CIDR notion. It must be contained by the address space of the virtual network.

- **Service endpoints (Preview)**: It can be used in securing your traffic between some Azure services in Microsoft's backbone network. More information about it will be covered in `Chapter 2`, *Delving into Azure Virtual Networks*:

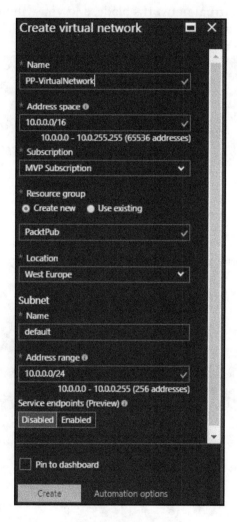

Figure 1.6: Creating a virtual network

5. Click on **Create**, and within a moment the virtual network will be created.

Adding address spaces to the virtual network

You can add other address spaces to the virtual network, and later those address spaces can be divided into subnets. To add another address space, follow these steps:

1. Navigate to the **Virtual networks** blade, and you will find that the virtual network you have created is already there, as shown in the following screenshot:

Figure 1.7: Displaying the created virtual networks

2. Click on the virtual network, and a new blade will pop up, as shown in the following screenshot:

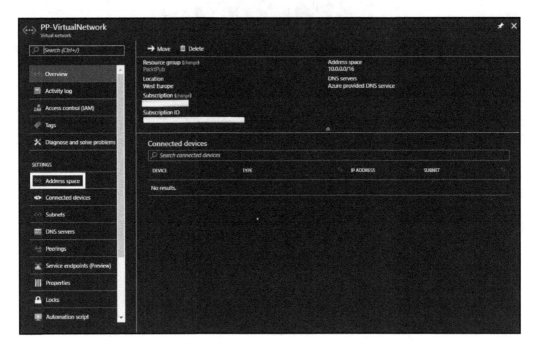

Figure 1.8: PP-Virtual Network overview

3. Then, you will navigate to **Address space**, wherein you will find all the address spaces of this virtual network, as shown in the following screenshot:

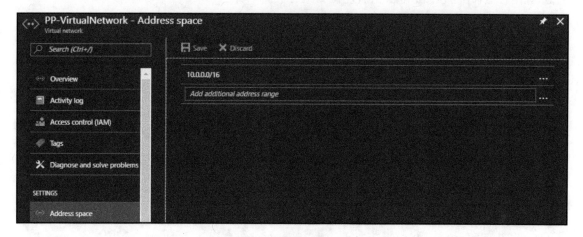

Figure 1.9: Address spaces of the virtual network

4. To add a new address space, you only need to hover over **Add additional address range**, and add the address space you would need, then click on **Save**, as shown in the following screenshot:

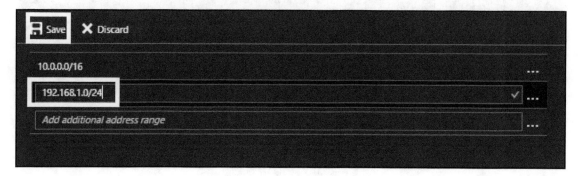

Figure 1.10: Adding new address space

5. Once you save the changes, the address space will be a part of the virtual network.

Adding subnets to the virtual network

There are two types of subnets in Azure VNet:

- **Subnet**: The normal form of subnets, which is the result of dividing the virtual network
- **Gateway subnet**: The subnet that acts as a gateway for communication with other networks

By default, you must specify at least one subnet while creating the virtual network, as discussed earlier. However, later you might need to have other subnets, and to do so, you have to follow these steps:

1. Navigate to the virtual network that you have created earlier and then go to **SETTINGS | Subnets**, as shown in the following screenshot:

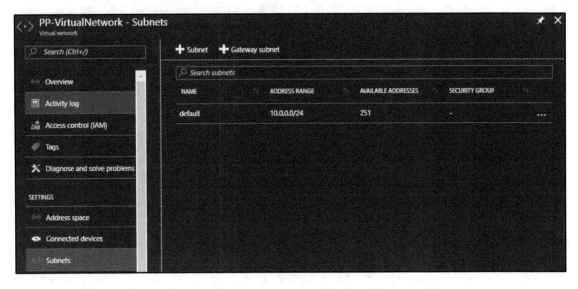

Figure 1.11: Virtual Network Subnets

2. Click on **Subnets**, and a new blade will be opened, where you need to specify the following:
   - **Name**: The name of the subnet.
   - **Address range (CIDR block)**: The subnet's address range in CIDR notation (considering that it must be contained by the address space of the virtual network).

- **Network security group**: This works like a firewall to filter what traffic that be allowed to flow in/out of the network. More information about this topic will be covered in `Chapter 2`, *Delving into Azure Virtual Networks*.
- **Route table**: You can expand the communication between multiple VNets by setting a route table. More information about this topic will be covered in `Chapter 4`, *Network Connectivity Scenarios in Azure*.
- **Service endpoints (Preview)**: As mentioned earlier, this can be used to let some Azure services communicate in Microsoft's backbone network. More information about it will be covered in `Chapter 2`, *Delving into Azure Virtual Networks*.

Figure 1.12: Adding subnets

3. Once you click on **OK**, the subnet will be added within a moment.

When specifying the subnet's address range, you must have noted that there are five reserved IPs. The first and the last IPs are reserved for protocol conformance known as *network and broadcast* in addition to three more IPs used for Azure services.

Creating the gateway subnet is no different than the normal subnet creation, except you cannot set the name of the gateway subnet, as shown in the following screenshot:

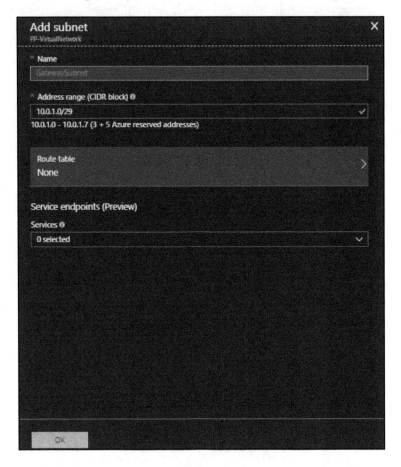

Figure 1.13: Adding gateway subnet

Every virtual network can only have one gateway subnet.

Azure VNet key points

While building your virtual network, you might need to consider the following points:

- You cannot add the following address spaces to your virtual network:
    - 224.0.0.0/4 (multicast)
    - 255.255.255.255/32 (broadcast)
    - 127.0.0.0/8 (loopback)
    - 169.254.0.0/16 (link-local)
    - 168.63.129.16/32 (internal DNS)
- You cannot connect virtual networks that have overlapped address spaces
- As a default limit, you can create 50 virtual networks per region per subscription, but it can be increased up to 1,000 virtual networks if you contact support
- As a default limit, you can create 1,000 subnets per virtual network, but it can be increased up to 10,000 subnets, if you contact support
- As a default limit, you can have 4,096 private IPs per virtual network, but it can be increased up to 8,192 if you contact support

Automating your tasks

It is no surprise that we commonly face repetitive and time-consuming tasks. For example, you might want to create multiple storage accounts. You would have to follow the previous guide multiple times to get your job done. This is why Microsoft supports its Azure services with multiple ways of automating most of the tasks that can be implemented in Azure. Throughout this book, two of the automation methods that Azure supports will be used.

Azure PowerShell

PowerShell is commonly used with most Microsoft products, and Azure is not less important than any of these products.

Mainly, you can use Azure PowerShell cmdlets to manage Azure Networking tasks, however, you should be aware that Microsoft Azure has two types of cmdlets, one for the ASM model, and another for the ARM model, which we will be using throughout this book.

The main difference between cmdlets of the ASM model and the ARM model is, there will be an RM added to the cmdlet of the current portal.

For example, if you want to create an ASM virtual network, you would use the following cmdlet:

```
New-AzureVirtualNetwork
```

But for the ARM model, you would use the following:

```
New-AzureRMVirtualNetwork
```

Most of the time this would be the case. But a few Cmdlets are totally different and some others don't even exist in the ASM model and do exist in the ARM model.

By default, you can use Azure PowerShell cmdlets in Windows PowerShell, but you will have to install its module first.

Installing the Azure PowerShell module

There are two ways of installing the Azure PowerShell module on Windows:

- Download and install the module from the following link: `https://www.microsoft.com/web/downloads/platform.aspx`
- Install the module from PowerShell Gallery

Installing the Azure PowerShell module from PowerShell Gallery

The following are the required steps to get Azure PowerShell installed:

1. Open PowerShell in an elevated mode.
2. To install the Azure PowerShell module for the current portal run the following cmdlet `Install-Module AzureRM`. If your PowerShell requires a NuGet provider you will be asked to agree to install it, and you will have to agree for the installation policy modification, as the repository is not available on your environment, as shown in the following screenshot:

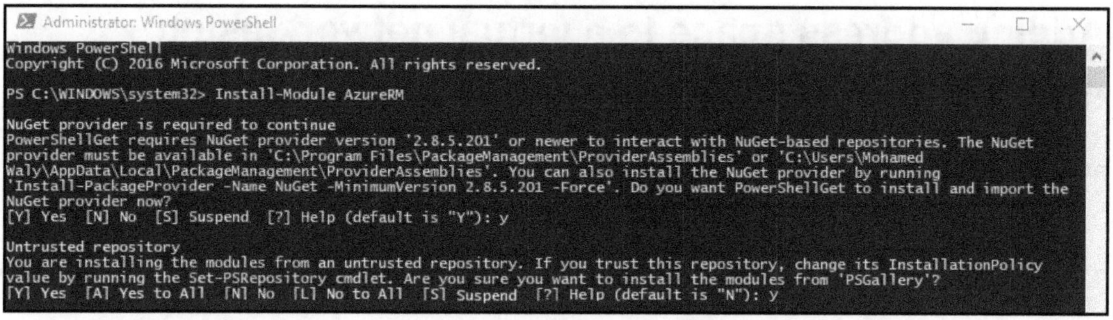

Figure 1.14 Installing the AzureRM PowerShell module

Creating a virtual network in Azure portal using PowerShell

To be able to run your PowerShell cmdlets against Azure successfully, you need to log in first to Azure using the following cmdlet:

```
Login-AzureRMAccount
```

Then, you will be prompted to enter the credentials of your Azure account. Voila! You are logged in and you can run Azure PowerShell cmdlets successfully.

To create an Azure VNet, you first need to create the subnets that will be attached to this virtual network. Therefore, let's get started by creating the subnets:

```
$NSubnet = New-AzureRMVirtualNetworkSubnetConfig –Name NSubnet –
AddressPrefix 192.168.1.0/24
$GWSubnet = New-AzureRMVirtualNetworkSubnetConfig –Name GatewaySubnet –
AddressPrefix 192.168.2.0/27
```

Now you are ready to create a virtual network by triggering the following cmdlet:

```
New-AzureRMVirtualNetwork –ResourceGroupName PacktPub –Location WestEurope
–Name PSVNet –AddressPrefix 192.168.0.0/16 –Subnet $NSubnet,$GWSubnet
```

Congratulations! You have your virtual network up and running with two subnets associated to it, one of them is a gateway subnet.

Adding address space to a virtual network using PowerShell

To add an address space to a virtual network, you need retrieve the virtual network first and store it in a variable by running the following cmdlet:

```
$VNet = Get-AzureRMVirtualNetwork -ResourceGroupName PacktPub -Name PSVNet
```

Then, you can add the address space by running the following cmdlet:

```
$VNet.AddressSpace.AddressPrefixes.Add("10.1.0.0/16")
```

Finally, you need to save the changes you have made by running the following cmdlet:

```
Set-AzureRmVirtualNetwork -VirtualNetwork $VNet
```

Azure CLI

Azure CLI is an open source, cross platform that supports implementing all the tasks you can do in Azure portal, with commands.

Azure CLI comes in two flavors:

- **Azure CLI 2.0**: Which supports only the current Azure portal
- **Azure CLI 1.0**: Which supports both portals

Throughout this book, we will be using Azure CLI 2.0, so let's get started with its installation.

Installing Azure CLI 2.0

Perform the following steps to install Azure CLI 2.0:

1. Download Azure CLI 2.0, from the following link: https://azurecliprod.blob.core.windows.net/msi/azure-cli-2.0.22.msi

2. Once downloaded, you can start the installation:

Figure 1.15: Installing Azure CLI 2.0

3. Once you click on **Install**, it will start to validate your environment to check whether it is compatible with it or not, then it starts the installation:

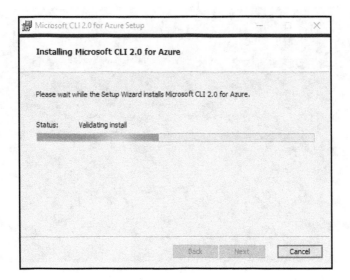

Figure 1.16: Installing Azure CLI 2.0

4. Once the installation completes, you can click on **Finish**, and you are good to go:

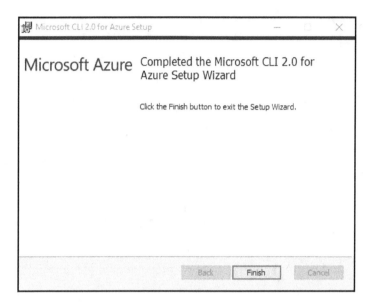

Figure 1.17: Installing Azure CLI 2.0

5. Once done, you can open cmd, and write az to access Azure CLI commands:

Figure 1.18: Opening the Azure CLI using CMD

Creating a virtual network using Azure CLI 2.0

To create a virtual network using Azure CLI 2.0, you have to follow these steps:

1. Log in to your Azure account using the following command `az login`, you have to open the URL that pops up on the CLI, and then enter the following code:

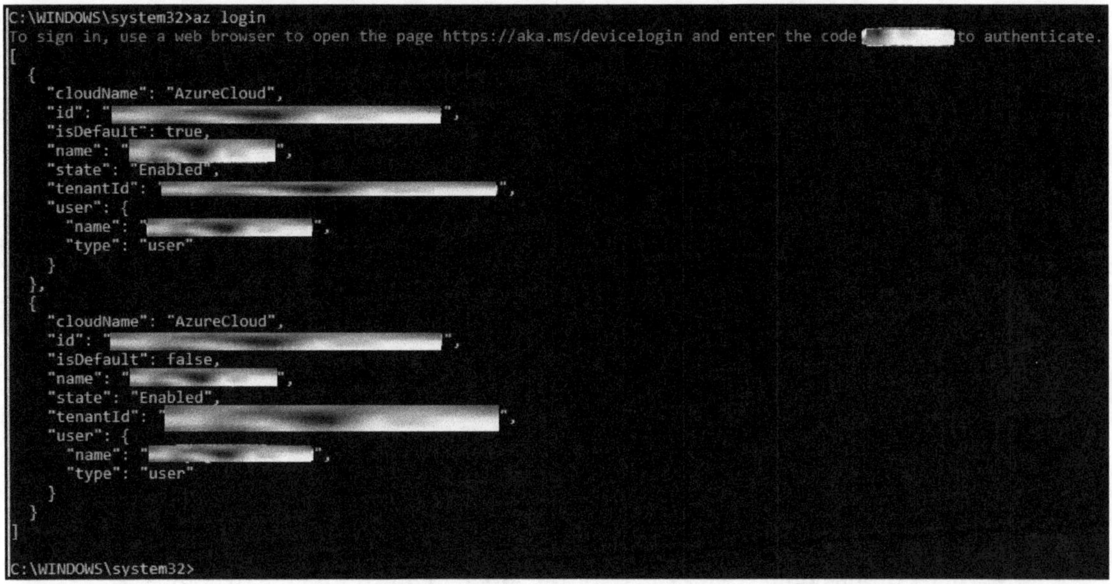

```
C:\WINDOWS\system32>az login
To sign in, use a web browser to open the page https://aka.ms/devicelogin and enter the code         to authenticate.
[
  {
    "cloudName": "AzureCloud",
    "id": "                              ",
    "isDefault": true,
    "name": "                ",
    "state": "Enabled",
    "tenantId": "                              ",
    "user": {
      "name": "                    ",
      "type": "user"
    }
  },
  {
    "cloudName": "AzureCloud",
    "id": "                              ",
    "isDefault": false,
    "name": "                ",
    "state": "Enabled",
    "tenantId": "                              ",
    "user": {
      "name": "                    ",
      "type": "user"
    }
  }
]
C:\WINDOWS\system32>
```

Figure 1.19: Logging in to Azure via Azure CLI 2.0

2. To create a new virtual network, you need to run the following command:

```
az network vnet create --name CLIVNet --resource-group PacktPub --
location westeurope --address-prefix 192.168.0.0/16 --subnet-name
s1 --subnet-prefix 192.168.1.0/24
```

Adding a gateway subnet to a virtual network using Azure CLI 2.0

To add a gateway subnet to a virtual network, you need to run the following command:

```
az network vnet subnet create --address-prefix 192.168.7.0/27 --name
GatewaySubnet --resource-group PacktPub --vnet-name CLIVNet
```

Adding an address space to a virtual network using Azure CLI 2.0

To add an address space to a virtual network, you can run the following command:

```
az network vnet update address-prefixes -add <Add JSON String>
```

Remember that you will need to add a JSON string that describes the address space.

Summary

So far, we have covered some preliminary subject matters regarding Azure generally, and Azure Networking specifically. Some things were not covered in detail, but detailed discussions will be raised in the coming chapters.

In the upcoming chapters, Azure networks architecture and more Azure networking services will be covered in detail. Therefore, the knowledge gained in this chapter is required for a better understanding of the coming chapters.

Questions

- Microsoft has data centers all over the globe in all continents (true/false)
- You can assign a single Azure resource to multiple resource groups (true/false)
- State three benefits of using the ARM model instead of the ASM model
- State the tools that can be used to automate Azure tasks
- What is the difference between address space and a subnet in terms of Azure networking?
- What is the difference between a subnet and gateway subnet in terms of Azure networking?
- Can you use 168.63.129.16/32 as an address space? Why/why not?

Further reading

For more information about virtual networks, you can check out the following link: `https:/` `/docs.microsoft.com/en-us/azure/virtual-network/virtual-networks-overview`.

2

Delving into Azure Virtual Networks

Introduction

This chapter will take you through the architecture of Azure **Virtual Network** (**VNet**). Then, Azure service endpoints will be introduced, and how to work with them.

Since Azure VNet works with almost all Azure services, you will be introduced to how Azure VNet integrates with Azure services, followed by virtual network peering, which will show you how to expand your connection to other virtual networks. After that, you will learn about best practices to secure your virtual networks in Azure. Finally, you will learn how to automate all the manual tasks implemented throughout the chapter.

Learning outcomes

The following topics will be covered in this chapter:

- Understanding Azure VNet architecture
- Azure VNet service endpoints
- Azure services integration with VMs
- Virtual network peering
- Securing Azure VNet
- Automating the tasks

Understanding Azure VNet architecture

Understanding a concept and learning how to do a specific task is very fulfilling for most people who are seeking to learn something. However, this section will take you beyond that and will introduce what is going on behind the scenes, what Microsoft uses to get its Azure networking to work properly, and so on.

Microsoft Azure mainly takes advantage of **Software-Defined Networking (SDN)** for the internal operations of Azure, but this is not the case for the case when the customers work with Azure as they are communicating with Azure via the internet most of the time, which is called the **edge**. In this part of the network, Microsoft uses physical networking.

Put simply, the concept of using virtual networks with subnets and virtual network gateways is running on the backbone of Azure. However, on the edge physical network devices, such as routers, switches, firewalls, and so on, are used.

Throughout the book, all of the SDN services, such as Azure Load Balancers, Traffic Manager, Application Gateway, and so on, will be covered.

Azure VNet service endpoints

Since Microsoft launched Azure, we communicate with most of the Azure services via the internet. For example, when you want to connect to Azure SQL databases, you can only connect with it via internet, but when using service endpoints you can connect it using an Azure VM taking the advantage of Microsoft backbone network.

So, what if you could communicate with Azure services using the Microsoft Azure backbone network. This would be interesting, right?

That is what virtual network service endpoints do. They create a direct connection to the service you want to communicate with via the virtual network where you have enabled service endpoints. Doing so will ensure that all the traffic between your data center and Azure service is done via the Microsoft network backbone.

At the time of writing, this feature in preview only supports Azure SQL Database and Azure Storage.

Why use VNet service endpoints?

VNet service endpoints are mainly used because they provide security. Using virtual network service endpoints eliminates the public internet access to your Azure resources, and it will only be allowed for the virtual network with service endpoints enabled for it.

Also, reserved public IPs are not needed any more, and last but not least, the management of virtual network service endpoints is very simple and straightforward, so it does not have a high management overhead.

Configuring service endpoints for Azure VNet

In `Chapter 1`, *Azure Virtual Networks 101*, you were able to enable service endpoints for the virtual network while creating it, as shown in the following screenshot:

Figure 2.1: Enabling service endpoints for a virtual network during creation

You can perform the following steps to configure it for the virtual network that was created in the previous chapter:

1. Navigate to the virtual network that was created in the previous chapter.
2. Scroll down and click on **Service endpoints (Preview)**, as shown in the following screenshot:

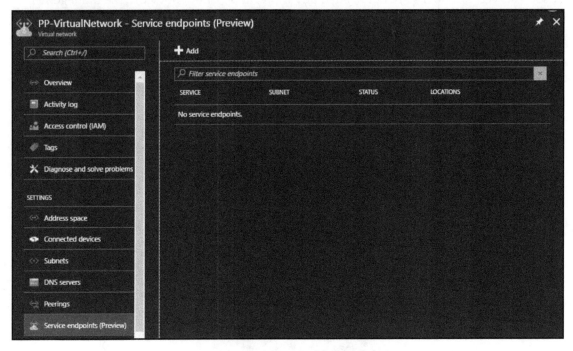

Figure 2.2: Virtual network service endpoints

3. To add a service endpoint, click on **Add**, and a new blade will pop up, as shown in the following screenshot:

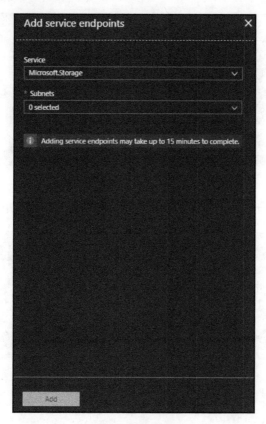

Figure 2.3: Add service endpoints

4. Click on the **Service** dropdown to select the service you want to create a service endpoint for, as shown in the following screenshot:

Figure 2.4: Selecting the service for which the service endpoint will be created

5. Once the service is selected, you need to specify the subnets where you want to apply the service endpoint, as shown in the following screenshot:

Figure 2.5: Selecting the subnet for the endpoint

6. Once you are done, click on **Add**, and it will be added within a short time:

Figure 2.6: Current service endpoints

7. To add a service endpoint for Azure SQL, you have to go through the same steps mentioned previously.

Azure VNet service endpoints key points

For a better understanding of Azure VNet service endpoints, you might need to consider the following key points:

- This feature cannot be enabled for virtual networks deployed with the ASM model, but it is supported for virtual networks deployed with the ARM model.
- This service endpoint cannot work with traffic from your on-premises environment.
- Using virtual network service endpoints will incur no charges.

- Make sure that there are no running tasks when you want to enable/disable service endpoints to a specific service (Azure Storage and Azure SQL Database) for a subnet.
- You cannot create multiple service endpoints for one service (Azure Storage and Azure SQL Database) on the same subnet. However, you can create multiple service endpoints for multiple services on the same subnet.
- You need to make sure that all Azure services for which you want to enable service endpoints for, exist with the virtual network on which the service endpoints are enabled in the same region.
- If you have storage accounts with **Geo-redundant storage (GRS)** or **Read-access geo-redundant storage (RA-GRS)** enabled, you do not have to worry because service endpoints can span across the region on which they are deployed and the paired region. However, ensure that the primary storage account exists on the region on which the virtual network is located.
- The virtual network with service endpoints enabled can be in another subscription, and it would still work with the service for which you want to enable service endpoints.

Azure services integration with virtual networks

At the time of writing, Microsoft provides a wide variety of services, such as Azure VMs, Service Fabric, HDInsight, Redis Cache, and so on.

Can you imagine using any of these services without communicating with it to either get your tasks done or manage it yourself?

Of course you cannot, because what is the point of buying these services then? That is why you will be using virtual networks to provide a communication method to most of your services.

Azure VNet can be integrated with other services, either by assigning your Azure service to a virtual network, as is the case in Azure VMs when you want to assign the VMs you are going to build to a specific virtual network, or by extending your virtual network to a specific service by using virtual network service endpoints.

Integrating Azure services with Azure VNet key benefits

Integrating Azure services with Azure VNet has many advantages. The following are some of them:

- Assigning different resources to the same subnet ensures that the communication between these services is done privately within the virtual network.
- You can communicate with Azure resources on-premise directly via its virtual network in case you have a site-to-site VPN or ExpressRoute configured in your environment.

> More information about connectivity scenarios between on-premises and Azure will be covered in `Chapter 4`, *Network Connectivity Scenarios in Azure*.

- By default, multiple virtual networks are isolated from each other. However, they can be peered together, allowing communication between resources in the different virtual networks.
- You are not responsible for managing virtual network service endpoints.
- Traffic can be controlled to/from the virtual network using **network security group** (**NSG**).

> More information about NSG will be covered later in this chapter.

Virtual network peering

I've been working with Azure since 2012 and guess what? I can confirm that you will be using more than one virtual network for all your Azure services and when you create another virtual network, a situation may arise when you would need to let the resources in each virtual network to communicate with each other.

As you know, by default, virtual networks are isolated and cannot communicate with each other. However, with virtual network, peering it is no longer an issue.

Configuring virtual network peering

Configuring virtual network peering is a very straightforward process. To do so, you can follow these steps:

1. Navigate to **Virtual networks**, and open the blade of one of the virtual networks that you want to peer.
2. Scroll down to **Peerings**, as shown in the following screenshot:

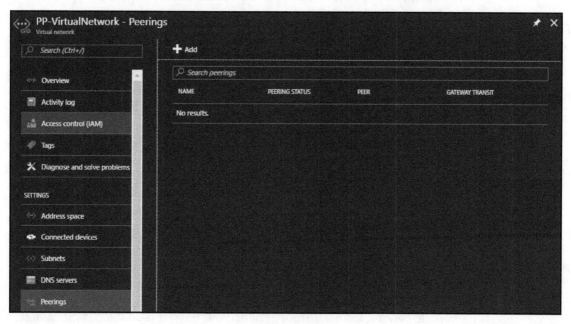

Figure 2.7: Virtual network peering

3. Click on **Add**, and a new blade will pop up, where you have to specify the following:

- **Name**: Give the peer a name.
- **Virtual network deployment model**: Specify whether you want to work with **Resource manager** or **Classic** model.
- **I know my resource ID**: Select this option to enter the resource ID of the virtual network you wish to peer with if you do not have read access to the virtual network or a subscription you want to peer with.
- **Subscription**: Select the subscription of the virtual network you wish to peer with.
- **Virtual network**: Specify the virtual network you wish to peer with.
- **Allow virtual network access**: Enable this option if you wish to allow communication between the two virtual networks. This allows the virtual network address space to be included as a part of the `VIRTUAL_NETWORK` tag.
- **Allow forwarded traffic**: This option allows the peer's forwarded traffic (traffic not originating from inside the peer virtual network) into your virtual network.
- **Allow gateway transit**: This option allows the peer virtual network to use your virtual network gateway. The virtual network cannot have a gateway configured, and must select **Use remote gateways** in its peering settings.
- **Use remote gateways**: Select this option if you wish to use your peer's virtual network gateway. The peer virtual network must have a gateway configured, as well as **Allow gateway transit** enabled. Only one peering in this virtual network can have this enabled. You cannot use this setting if you already have a gateway configured in your virtual network.

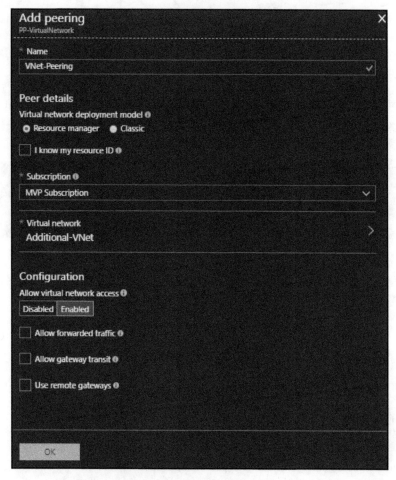

Figure 2.8: Configuring the peering

4. Once you are done, you can see that the peer has been created, as shown in the following screenshot:

Figure 2.9: The created peer

5. As you can see in the previous screenshot, the **PEERING STATUS** is **Initiated**, and that means you are only done with the first part. Therefore, you need to navigate to the peered virtual network and repeat the same steps for the peer creation.

6. Once you are done with repeating the process on the peered virtual network, the **PEERING STATUS** should be turned into **Connected**, which means everything is going fine, and you can communicate successfully with resources from any virtual network peer, as shown in the following screenshot:

Figure 2.10: Peering status change

7. By now and based on the settings you have specified during the peering configuration, the traffic would follow between the two virtual networks.

Virtual network peering key points

For a better understanding of virtual network peering, you need to consider the following key points:

- Peered virtual networks do not need any encryption, public internet, or event gateways, as they use the Microsoft backbone network.
- Using virtual network peering provides a low-latency, high bandwidth connection between the resources in each virtual network.
- Virtual network peering can be used to migrate resources from one subscription/region to another, because Microsoft Azure supports the concept of peering virtual networks in different subscriptions/regions.

Peering for virtual networks located in different regions is currently in preview and is only available for the following regions: US West Central, Canada Central, and US West 2. Also, you need to register your subscription first to try this feature, otherwise, the peer creation will fail. For more information about the subscription registration for this feature, you can check out the following link: `https://docs.microsoft.com/en-us/azure/virtual-network/virtual-network-create-peering#register`.

- Virtual networks with different deployment models can be peered together.
- No disturbance occurs during the peering process. In other words, you can expect no downtime.
- Ensure that the peered virtual networks have non-overlapping IP address spaces.
- Ensure that you have added all the needed address spaces for your virtual networks before peering them, because once the peer is created, you can no longer add any address spaces.
- Do not expect a transitive relationship among the virtual networks. In other words, if you have virtual network 1, which is peered to virtual network 2, and virtual network B is peered to virtual network 3, that does not mean virtual network 1 and virtual network 3 are peered.
- If the peering status changed to **Disconnected**, that means the peering of one of the peered virtual networks has been deleted.

Securing Azure VNet

The most common question that anyone asks when they buy a service is, can it be secured? The answer to that question in this case is, absolutely yes.

Besides the security Microsoft provides for Azure from its side, there is some configuration that you can do from your side to increase the level of security to your virtual network.

For a higher level of security, you can use the following:

- **NSG**: It is like a firewall that controls the inbound and outbound traffic by specifying which traffic is allowed to flow to/from the NIC/subnet
- **Distributed denial of service (DDoS) protection**: It is used to prevent DDoS attacks and at the time of writing is in preview

NSG

NSG controls the flow of traffic by specifying which traffic is allowed to enter or exit the network.

Creating NSG

Creating an NSG is a pretty straightforward process. To do it, you need to follow these steps:

1. Navigate to Azure portal, and search for `network security groups`, as shown in the following screenshot:

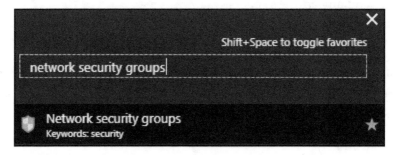

Figure 2.13: Searching for network security groups

2. Once you have clicked on it, a new blade will be opened wherein all the created NSGs are located, as shown in the following screenshot:

Figure 2.12: Network security groups blade

3. Click on **Add** and a new blade will pop up, where you have to specify the following:

  - **Name**: The name of the NSG
  - **Subscription**: The subscription, which will be charged for NSG usage
  - **Resource group**: The resource group within which the NSG will be located as a resource
  - **Location**: The region where this resource will be created

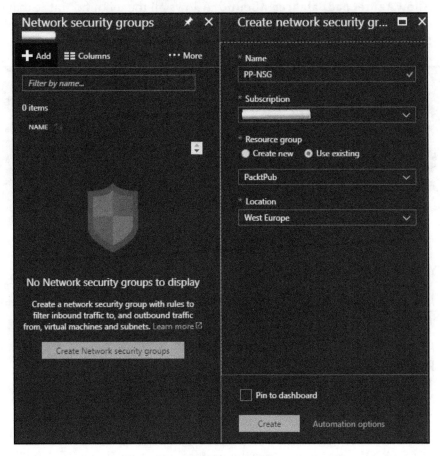

Figure 2.13: Creating an NSG

4. Once you have clicked on **Create**, the NSG will be created within seconds.

Inbound security rules

By default, all the subnets and NICs that are not associated with NSG have all the inbound traffic allowed and once they are associated with an NSG, the following inbound security rules are assigned to them as they are a default part of any NSG:

- **AllowVnetInBound**: Allows all the inbound traffic that comes from a virtual network
- **AllowAzureLoadBalancerInBound**: Allows all the inbound traffic that comes from Load Balancer
- **DenyAllInbound**: Denies all the inbound traffic that comes from any source

PRIORITY	NAME	PORT	PROTOCOL	SOURCE	DESTINATION	ACTION	
65000	AllowVnetInBound	Any	Any	VirtualNetwork	VirtualNetwork	✅ Allow	...
65001	AllowAzureLoadBalancerInBou...	Any	Any	AzureLoadBala...	Any	✅ Allow	...
65500	DenyAllInBound	Any	Any	Any	Any	⊗ Deny	...

Figure 2.14: Default inbound security rules

As shown in the previous screenshot, the rule consists of some properties, such as **PRIORITY**, **NAME**, **PORT**, and so on.

It is important to understand what these properties mean for a better understanding of security rules. So, let's go ahead and explain them:

- **PRIORITY**: A number assigned to each rule to specify which rule has a higher priority than the other. The lower the number, the higher the priority. You can specify a priority with any number between 100 and 4096.
- **NAME**: The name of the rule. The same name cannot be reused within the same network security group.
- **PORT**: The allowed port through which the traffic will flow to the network.
- **PROTOCOL**: Specify whether the protocol you are using is TCP or UDP.
- **SOURCE** and **DESTINATION**: The source can be any, an IP address range, or a service tag.

You can remove the default rules by clicking on **Default rules**.

You can customize your own inbound rules, by following these steps:

1. On the **Inbound security rules** blade, click on **Add.**
2. A new blade will pop up, where you have to specify the following:
   - **Source**: The source can be **Any**, an IP address range, or a service tag. It specifies the incoming traffic from a specific source IP address range that will be allowed or denied by this rule.
   - **Source port ranges**: You can provide a single port, such as 80, a port range, such as 1024 - 65535, or a comma-separated list of single ports and/or port ranges, such as 80, 1024 - 65535. This specifies on which ports traffic will be allowed or denied by this rule. Provide an asterisk (*) to allow traffic on any port.
   - **Destination**: The destination can be **Any**, an IP address range, or a virtual network. It specifies the outing traffic to a specific destination IP address range that will be allowed or denied by this rule.
   - **Destination port ranges**: What applies for the source port ranges, applies for the destination port ranges.
   - **Protocol**: It can be **Any**, **TCP**, or **UDP**.
   - **Action**: Whether to **Allow** the rule or to **Deny** it.
   - **Priority**: As mentioned earlier, the lower the number, the higher the priority. The priority number must be between 100 - 4096.
   - **Name**: The name of the rule.
   - **Description**: The description of the rule, which will help you to differentiate between the rules.

3. In our scenario, I want to allow all the incoming connections to access a website published on a web server located in a virtual network, as shown in the following screenshot:

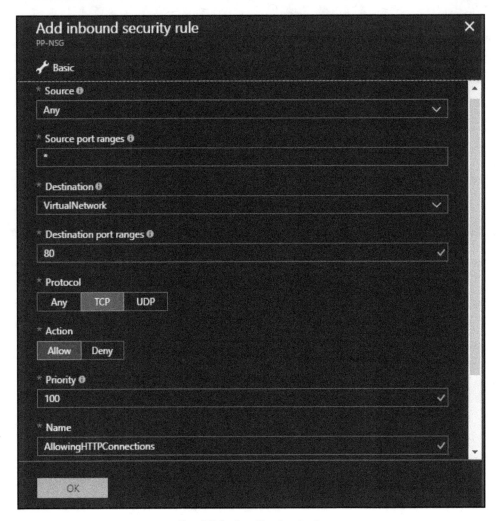

Figure 2.15: Creating an inbound security rule

4. Once you click on **OK**, the rule will be created.

Outbound security rules

Outbound security rules are no different than inbound security rules, except inbound rules are meant for inbound traffic and outbound rules are meant for outbound traffic. Otherwise, everything else is similar.

Associating the NSG

Once you have the NSG created, you can associate it to either an NIC or a subnet.

Associating the NSG to an NIC

To associate the NSG to an NIC, you need to follow these steps:

1. Navigate to the **Network security groups** that you have created and then select **Network interfaces,** as shown in the following screenshot:

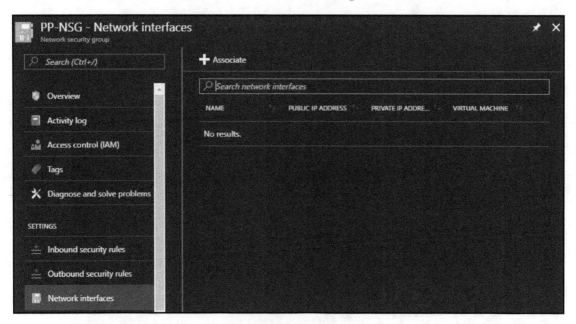

Figure 2.16: Associated NICs to an NSG

2. Click on **Associate.**

3. A new blade will pop up, from which you need to select the NIC that you want to associate with the NSG, as shown in the following screenshot:

Figure 2.17: NICs to be associated to the NSG

4. Voila! You are done.

Associating the NSG to a subnet

To associate the NSG to a subnet, you need to follow these steps:

1. Navigate to the **Network security groups** that you have created and then select **Subnets,** as shown in the following screenshot:

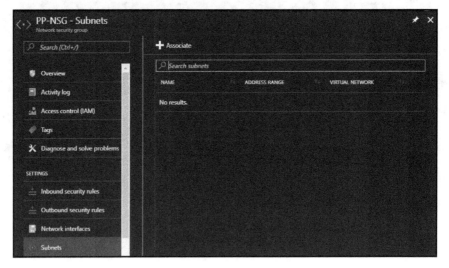

Figure 2.18: Associated subnets to an NSG

2. Click on **Associate.**

3. A new blade will pop up, where you have to specify the virtual network within which the subnet exists, as shown in the following screenshot:

Figure 2.19: Choosing the VNet within which the subnet exists

4. Then, you need to specify which subnet of the VNet you want to associate the NSG to, as shown in the following screenshot:

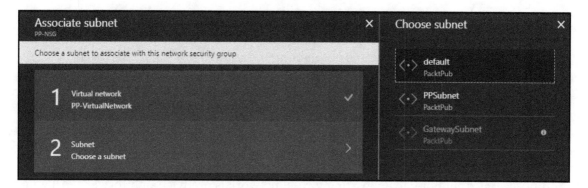

Figure 2.20: Selecting the subnet to which the NSG will be associated

5. Once the subnet is selected, click on **OK**, and it will take some seconds to get it associated to the NSG.

Azure DDoS protection

DDoS attacks have spread out lately, by exhausting the application and making it unavailable for use, and you can expect an attack of that type any time. Recently, Microsoft announced the support of Azure DDoS protection as a service for protecting Azure resources, such as Azure VMs, Load Balancers, and Application Gateways.

Azure DDoS protection comes in two flavors:

- **Basic**: This type has been around for a while as it is already enabled for Azure services to mitigate DDoS attacks. It incurs no charges.
- **Standard**: This flavor comes with more enhancements that mitigate attacks, especially for Azure VNet.

At the time of writing, Azure DDoS protection standard is in preview and it is not available at the portal, you need to request it by filling a out a form that is available at the following link: `https://forms.office.com/Pages/ResponsePage.aspx?id=v4j5cvGGr0GRqy180BHbR6OXgXv2dvJMjGuqdiRkkHNUMzJTUkZHUjhLU0QzQktGTVBVSjA3SkhUSy4u`.

Automating the tasks

Finally, we have reached the point of automating the manual tasks that have been implemented so far.

Adding a service endpoint to an existing virtual network using PowerShell

Adding a service endpoint to an existing virtual network is pretty straightforward. All you need to do is run the following cmdlet:

```
Get-AzureRmVirtualNetwork -ResourceGroupName PacktPub -Name PSVNet | Set-
AzureRmVirtualNetworkSubnetConfig -Name NSubnet  -AddressPrefix
"192.168.1.0/24" -ServiceEndpoint "Microsoft.Storage" | Set-
AzureRmVirtualNetwork
```

Adding a service endpoint to an existing virtual network using Azure CLI

To add a service endpoint to an existing virtual network using Azure CLI, you need to run the following command:

```
az network vnet subnet update -g PacktPub -n s1 --vnet-name CLIVNet --
service-endpoints Microsoft.Storage
```

Creating virtual network peering using PowerShell

First off, you need to retrieve the virtual network information and store it in a variable using the following cmdlet:

```
$VNet1 = Get-AzureRmVirtualNetwork -ResourceGroupName PacktPub -Name PSVNet
$VNet2 = Get-AzureRmVirtualNetwork -ResourceGroupName PacktPub -Name
PSVNet2
```

Then, you will add the peer from vnet1 to vnet2 by running the following cmdlet:

```
Add-AzureRmVirtualNetworkPeering -Name PSVNetPeer -VirtualNetwork $vnet1 -
RemoteVirtualNetworkId $vnet2.Id
```

After that, you will add the peer from vnet2 to vnet1 by running the following cmdlet:

```
Add-AzureRmVirtualNetworkPeering -Name PSVNetPeer -VirtualNetwork $vnet2 -
RemoteVirtualNetworkId $vnet1.Id
```

Now, you are done and have the peer in a connected state.

Creating virtual network peering using Azure CLI

First off, you need to retrieve the virtual network ID using the following command for the peered VNet and store it in a variable to be used later:

```
$vnet1Id=$(az network vnet show --resource-group PacktPub --name CLIVNet --
query id --out tsv)
$vnet2Id=$(az network vnet show --resource-group PacktPub --name CLIVNet2 -
-query id --out tsv)
```

Then, you can create the peer from vnet1 to vnet2 by running the following command:

```
az network vnet peering create --name CLIVNetPeering --resource-group
PacktPub --vnet-name CLIVNet --remote-vnet-id $vnet2Id --allow-vnet-access
```

Now, you can finalize that by creating the peer from vnet1 to vnet2 by running the following command:

```
az network vnet peering create --name CLIVNetPeering --resource-group
PacktPub --vnet-name CLIVNet2 --remote-vnet-id $vnet1Id --allow-vnet-access
```

Creating NSG using PowerShell

First off, you need to create a security rule and to do it, you need to run the following cmdlet:

```
$InboundRule = New-AzureRmNetworkSecurityRuleConfig -Name AllowingHTTP -
Description "Allow HTTP" -Access Allow -Protocol Tcp -Direction Inbound -
Priority 100 -SourceAddressPrefix Internet -SourcePortRange * -
DestinationAddressPrefix * -DestinationPortRange 80
```

Then, you can create the NSG with the previous rule added to it by running the following cmdlet:

```
$NSG = New-AzureRmNetworkSecurityGroup -ResourceGroupName PacktPub -
Location westeurope -Name PSNSG -SecurityRules $InboundRule
```

Creating NSG using Azure CLI

Unlike PowerShell, you can create an NSG by running one command at Azure CLI, shown as follows:

```
az network nsg rule create --resource-group PacktPub --nsg-name CLINSG --
name AllowHTTP --access Allow --protocol Tcp --direction Inbound --priority
150 --source-address-prefix Internet --source-port-range "*" --destination-
address-prefix "*" --destination-port-range 80
```

Associating NSG with a subnet using PowerShell

To associate the NSG that has been created earlier to a subnet, you can run the following cmdlet:

```
Get-AzureRmVirtualNetwork -ResourceGroupName PacktPub -Name PSVNet| Set-
AzureRmVirtualNetworkSubnetConfig -VirtualNetwork PSVNet -Name NSubnet -
AddressPrefix 192.168.1.0/24 -NetworkSecurityGroup $NSG
```

Then, you need to save your configuration by running the following cmdlet:

```
Set-AzureRmVirtualNetwork -VirtualNetwork PSVNet
```

Associating NSG with a subnet using Azure CLI

To attach the NSG that was created earlier to a subnet using Azure CLI, you can run the following command:

```
az network vnet subnet update --vnet-name CLIVNet --name S1--resource-group
PacktPub--network-security-group CLINSG
```

Summary

This chapter has covered some of the most interesting points regarding the architecture of Azure VNet and how it integrates with other Azure services. Not only that, but it also introduced some of the hottest and newest features, such as service endpoints and DDoS protection. Also, best practices for securing your environment using NSG were covered.

Based on the acquired information from this chapter, we will move forward to the next chapter and apply all that has been covered so far into how virtual networks work with Azure VMs.

Questions

- Service Endpoints provide high bandwidth and low latency as they create a fast connection to Azure services over the internet (true/false).
- You cannot peer virtual networks with different deployment models (true/false).
- Traffic can be controlled using NSG (true/false).
- What are the Azure services that are currently supported to work with service endpoints?
- What are the types of Azure DDoS protection?
- State and explain the three statuses of peering.
- Write a PowerShell script that creates two virtual networks with two subnets for each. Then, create a virtual network peering between these two virtual networks.

Further reading

You can check out the following links for more information on the topics covered in this chapter:

- **Learning Microsoft Azure Storage**: https://www.packtpub.com/big-data-and-business-intelligence/learning-microsoft-azure-storage
- **NSG**: https://docs.microsoft.com/en-us/azure/virtual-network/security-overview
- **Azure DDoS protection**: https://docs.microsoft.com/en-us/azure/virtual-network/ddos-protection-overview
- **Required permissions for accessing other subscriptions**: https://docs.microsoft.com/en-us/azure/virtual-network/create-peering-different-deployment-models-subscriptions#permissions
- **VPN gateway for peering virtual networks in different subscriptions**: https://docs.microsoft.com/en-us/azure/vpn-gateway/vpn-gateway-about-vpngateways?toc=%2fazure%2fvirtual-network%2ftoc.json#V2V
- **Configuring Azure Storage firewalls and virtual networks**: https://docs.microsoft.com/en-us/azure/storage/common/storage-network-security

3

Azure Network for VMs

Introduction

This chapter covers one of the most popular Azure services: Azure VMs. As well as looking at how Azure VMs work with Azure networking, this chapter will introduce Azure VMs and their types. We will then look into how you create Azure VMs, and how they relate to Azure Networks. Finally, we will automate all the manual tasks that were previously manually implemented.

Learning outcomes

In this chapter, the following topics will be covered:

- Introducing Azure VMs
- Creating and configuring networking for Azure VMs
- Automating tasks

Azure VMs

Azure **Virtual Machines** (**VMs**) is one of the oldest and most used services in Azure. Azure VMs has witnessed considerable development over the years; as a result, you can now have an Azure VM on the most popular operating systems. At the time of writing, Azure VMs is supported by a variety of operating systems that include, but are not limited to, Windows, Linux, Unix, and FreeBSD.

Azure VMs follows the **infrastructure as a service (IaaS)** model, so when using it you will be responsible for managing and configuring everything within the VM. You will not be responsible for managing and configuring the underlying hardware layer, however.

Azure VMs series

Azure VMs are available in different series, with each series demanding different specifications in order to fulfil the scenarios you want to deploy:

- **A-series**: This series is most commonly used in development and test scenarios
- **D-series**: This series has a fast CPU and **solid-state drive (SSD)** disks, and is most commonly used for general-purpose computing, such as relational databases, and every application that requires high IOPs
- **F-series**: This series targets applications that require intensive compute power, such as web servers
- **G-series**: This series targets applications that require high memory and fast storage, such as ERP, and SAP solutions
- **H-series**: This series has very high compute capabilities, and might fit in scenarios that require high performance, such as analytics
- **L-series**: This series is dedicated to applications that require low latency, high throughput, high IOPs, and large size disks, such as NoSQL databases
- **N-series**: This series has high GPU capabilities, and fits scenarios such as video editing, graphics rendering, and so on
- **B-series**: This series provides the lowest cost of any exciting size with flexible CPU usage; it mainly targets web servers, small databases, and development/test environments
- **M-series**: This series provides the biggest VM sizes in Azure at the time of writing; this series is a better fit for large in-memory workloads, such as SAP HANA and SQL Hekaton.

For further information about Azure VMs series and any upcoming series, you can check out the following page: https://azure.microsoft.com/en-us/pricing/details/virtual-machines/series/.

Azure VMs statuses

For a better understanding of how Azure VMs work, you need to know the statuses of the VMs.

State	Description
Running	The VM is running and you get charged for usage as usual
Stopped	The VM is shut down by Windows/Linux, but you still get charged for the VM, as it is still deployed to the same physical host and resources are still reserved for it
Stopped (Deallocated)	The VM is stopped by the stop button on the VM plane via the Azure portal; this state will cost the user no charges, except for the storage of the VM

At the moment there are two billing models available: Pay-As-You-Go and Reserved Instances.

- **Pay-As-You-Go**: This model enables you to pay for the VMs' usage as long as you are using them. In this model, Microsoft charges by the minute, so if you have used a VM for 61 minutes, for example, you will only pay for those 61 minutes.
- **Reserved Instances**: This model enables you to reserve a VM for 1, 2, or 3 years, which offers a high cost reduction compared to the Pay-As-You-Go model. The cost savings can be up to 82%.

 For more information about Reserved Instances, you can check out the following page: https://azure.microsoft.com/en-us/pricing/reserved-vm-instances/.

At the time of writing, Microsoft has two **Service Level Agreements** (**SLAs**) for Azure VMs, they are as follows:

- Two or more VMs within the same availability set have 99.95% availability to one VM guaranteed
- Using a single VM that uses Premium Storage will provide at least 99.9% availability

To stay updated on Microsoft SLAs for Azure VMs, check the following page: `https://azure.microsoft.com/en-us/support/legal/sla/virtual-machines/v1_6/`.

Creating and configuring Azure VMs

Creating an Azure VM is a very straightforward process – all you have to do is follow the given steps:

1. Navigate to the Azure portal and search for `Virtual Machines`, as shown in the following screenshot:

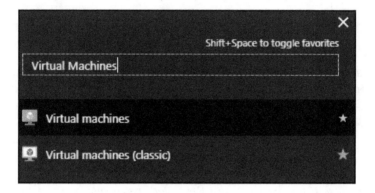

Figure 3.1: Searching for Virtual Machines

2. Once the VM blade is opened, you can click on **+Add** to create a new VM, as shown in the following screenshot:

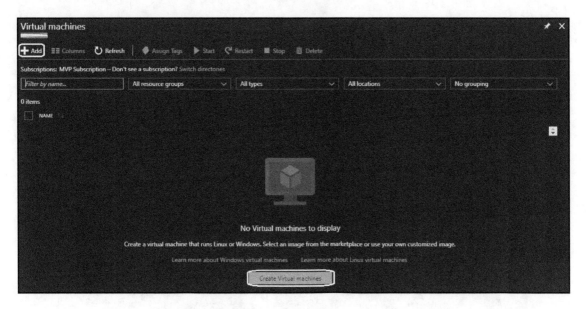

Figure 3.2: Virtual Machines blade

3. Once you have clicked on **+Add**, a new blade will pop up where you have to search for and select the desired OS for the VM, as shown in the following screenshot:

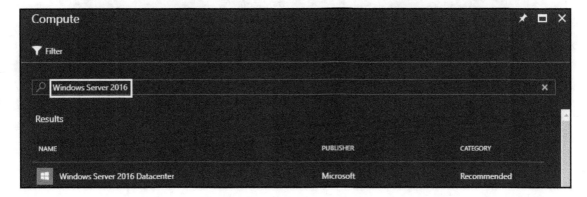

Figure 3.3: Searching for Windows Server 2016 OS for the VM

4. Once the OS is selected, you need to select the deployment model, whether that be **Resource Manager** or **Classic**, as shown in the following screenshot:

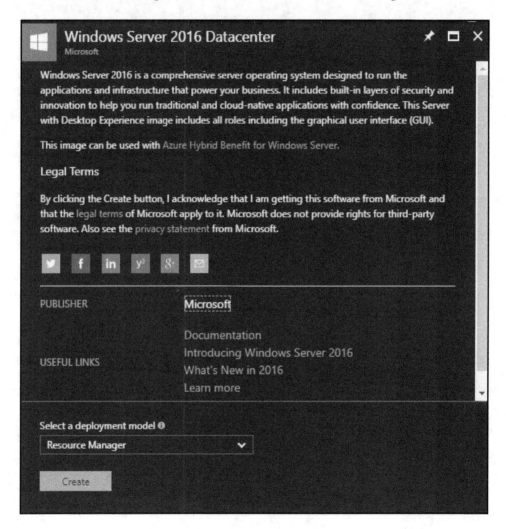

Figure 3.4: Selecting the deployment model

5. Once the deployment model is selected, a new blade will pop up where you have to specify the following:
    - **Name**: Specify the name of the VM.
    - **VM disk type**: Specify whether the disk type will be **SSD** or **HDD**. Consider that **SSD** will offer consistent, low-latency performance, but will incur more charges. Note that this option is not available for the **Classic** model in this blade, but is available in the **Configure optional features** blade.
    - **User name**: Specify the username that will be used to log on the VM.
    - **Password**: Specify the password, which must be between 12 and 123 characters long and must contain three of the following: one lowercase character, one uppercase character, one number, and one special character that is not \ or –.
    - **Subscription**: This specifies the subscription that will be charged for the VM usage.
    - **Resource group**: This specifies the resource group within which the VM will exist.
    - **Location**: Specify the location in which the VM will be created. It is recommended that you select the nearest location to you.
    - **Save money**: Here, you specify whether you own Windows Server Licenses with active Software Assurance (SA). If you do, Azure Hybrid Benefit is recommended to save compute costs.

For more information about Azure Hybrid Benefit, you can check out the following page: `https://docs.microsoft.com/en-us/azure/virtual-machines/windows/hybrid-use-benefit-licensing`.

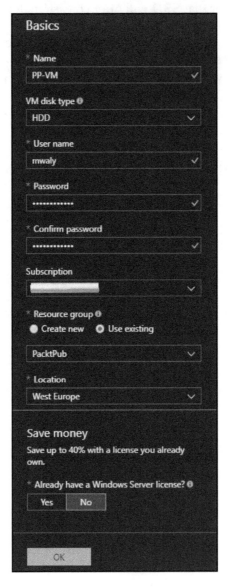

Figure 3.5: Configure the VM basic settings

6. Once you have clicked on **OK**, a new blade will pop up where you have to specify the VM size so that the VMs series can select the one that will fulfil your needs, as shown in the following screenshot:

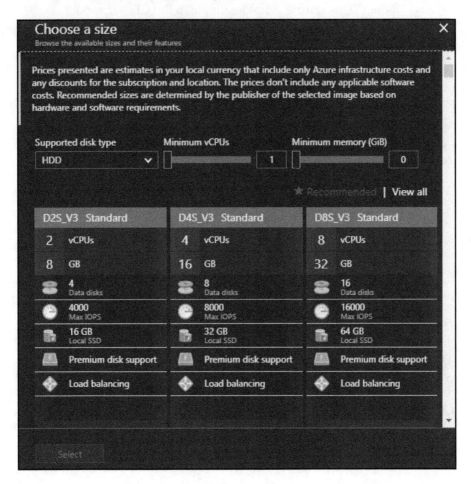

Figure 3.6: Select the VM size

7. Once the VM size has been specified, you need to specify the following settings:
   - **Availability set**: This option provides **High availability** for the VM by setting the VMs within the same application and availability set. Here, the VMs will be in different fault and update domains (which has been discussed in the table in `Chapter 1`, *Azure Virtual Networks 101*), granting the VMs high availability (up to 99.95% of Azure SLA).

- **Use managed disks**: Enable this feature to have Azure automatically manage the availability of disks to provide data redundancy and fault tolerance without creating and managing storage accounts on your own. This setting is not available in the **Classic** model.
- **Virtual network**: Specify the virtual network to which you want to assign the VM.
- **Subnet**: Select the subnet within the virtual network that you specified earlier to assign the VM to.
- **Public IP address**: Either select an existing public IP address or create a new one.
- **Network security group (firewall)**: Select the NSG you want to assign to the VM NIC. This is called **endpoints** in the **Classic** model.
- **Extensions**: You can add more features to the VM using extensions, such as configuration management, antivirus protection, and so on.
- **Auto-shutdown**: Specify whether you want to shut down your VM daily or not; if you do, you can set a schedule. Considering that this option will help you saving compute cost especially for dev and test scenarios. This is not available in the **Classic** model.
- **Notification before shutdown**: Check this if you enabled **Auto-shutdown** and want to subscribe for notifications before the VM shuts down. This is not available in the **Classic** model.
- **Boot diagnostics**: This captures serial console output and screenshots of the VM running on a host to help diagnose start up issues.
- **Guest OS diagnostics**: This obtains metrics for the VM every minute; you can use these metrics to create alerts and stay informed of your applications.
- **Diagnostics storage account**: This is where metrics are written, so you can analyze them with your own tools.

Figure 3.7: Specify more settings for the VM

Enabling **Boot diagnostics** and **Guest diagnostics** will incur more charges, since the diagnostics will need a dedicated storage account to store their data.

8. Finally, once you are done with its settings, Azure will validate those you have specified and summarize them, as shown in the following screenshot:

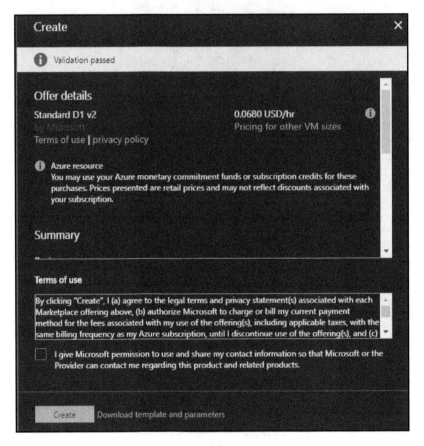

Figure 3.8: VM Settings Summary

9. Once clicked on, **Create** the VM will start the creation process, and within minutes the VM will be created.

10. Once the VM is created, you can navigate to the **Virtual Machines** blade to open the VM that has been created, as shown in the following screenshot:

Figure 3.9: The created VM overview

11. To connect to the VM, click on **Connect**, where a pre-configured RDP file with the required VM information will be downloaded.

12. Open the RDP file. You will be asked to enter the username and password you specified for the VM during its configuration, as shown in the following screenshot:

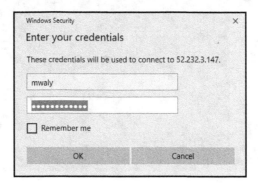

Figure 3.10: Entering the VM credentials

13. Voila! You should now be connected to the VM.

Azure VMs networking

There are many networking configurations that can be done for the VM. You can add additional NICs, change the private IP address, set a private or public IP address to be either static or dynamic, and you can change the inbound and outbound security rules.

Adding inbound and outbound rules

Adding inbound and outbound security rules to the VM NIC is a very simple process; all you need to do is follow these steps:

1. Navigate to the desired VM.
2. Scroll down to **Networking**, under **SETTINGS**, as shown in the following screenshot:

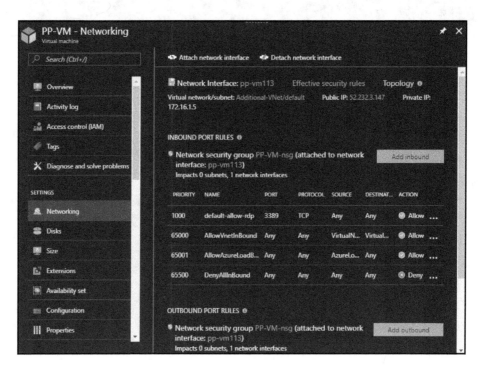

Figure 3.11: VM networking settings

3. To add inbound and outbound security rules, you have to click on either **Add inbound** or **Add outbound**.

4. Once clicked on, a new blade will pop up where you have to specify settings using the following fields:

   - **Service**: The service specifies the destination protocol and port range for this rule. Here, you can choose a predefined service, such as RDP or SSH, or provide a custom port range.
   - **Port ranges**: Here, you need to specify a single port, a port range, or a comma-separated list of single ports or port ranges.
   - **Priority**: Here, you enter the desired priority value. As mentioned in the *Securing Azure Virtual Networks* section of `Chapter 2`, *Delving into Azure Virtual Networks*, the lower the number, the higher the priority.
   - **Name**: Specify a name for the rule here.
   - **Description**: Write a description for the rule that relates to it here.

Figure 3.12: Adding an inbound rule

5. Once you have clicked **OK**, the rule will be applied. Note that the same process applies when adding an outbound rule.

Adding an additional NIC to the VM

Adding an additional NIC starts from the same blade as adding inbound and outbound rules. To add an additional NIC, you have to follow the given steps:

1. Before adding an additional NIC to the VM, you need to make sure that the VM is in a **Stopped (Deallocated)** status.
2. Navigate to **Networking** on the desired VM.
3. Click on **Attach network interface**, and a new blade will pop up. Here, you have to either create a network interface or select an existing one. If you are selecting an existing interface, simply click on **OK** and you are done. If you are creating a new interface, click on **Create network interface**, as shown in the following screenshot:

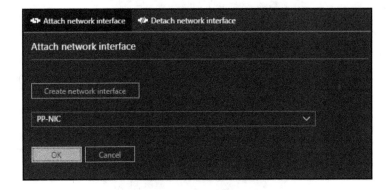

Figure 3.13: Attaching network interface

4. A new blade will pop up where you have to specify the following:

   - **Name**: The name of the new NIC.
   - **Virtual network**: This field will be grayed out because you cannot attach a VM's NIC to different virtual networks.
   - **Subnet**: Select the desired subnet within the virtual network.
   - **Private IP address assignment**: Specify whether you want to allocate this IP dynamically or statically.
   - **Network security group**: Specify an NSG to be assigned to this

NIC.

- **Private IP address (IPv6)**: If you want to assign an IPv6 to this NIC, check this setting.
- **Subscription**: This field will be grayed out because you cannot have a VM's NIC in a different subscription.
- **Resource group**: Specify the resource group to which the NIC will exist.
- **Location**: This field will be grayed out because you cannot have VM NICs in different locations.

Figure 3.14: Specify the NIC settings

5. Once you are done, click **Create**.

6. Once the network interface is created, you will return to the previous blade. Here, you need to specify the NIC you just created and click on **OK**, as shown in the following screenshot:

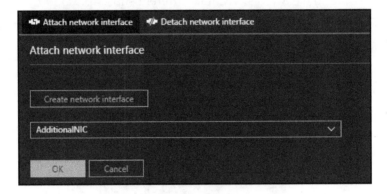

Figure 3.15: Attaching the NIC

Configuring the NICs

The **Network Interface Cards** (**NICs**) include some configuration that you might be interested in. They are as follows:

1. To navigate to the desired NIC, you can search for the `network interfaces` blade, as shown in the following screenshot:

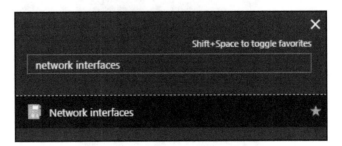

Figure 3.16: Searching for network interfaces blade

24444

2. Then, the blade will pop up, from which you can select the desired NIC, as shown in the following screenshot:

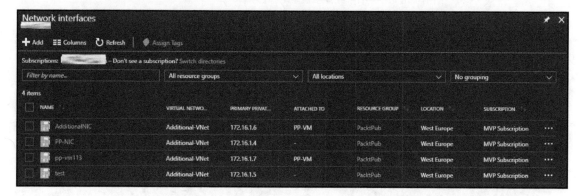

Figure 3.17: Select the desired NIC

3. You can also navigate back to the VM via | **Networking** | and then click on the desired NIC, as shown in the following screenshot:

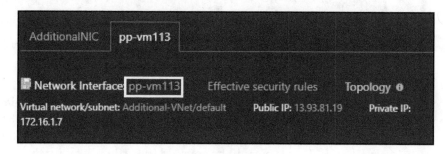

Figure 3.18: The VM NIC

4. To configure the NIC, you need to follow the given steps:
   1. Once the NIC blade is opened, navigate to **IP configurations**, as shown in the following screenshot:

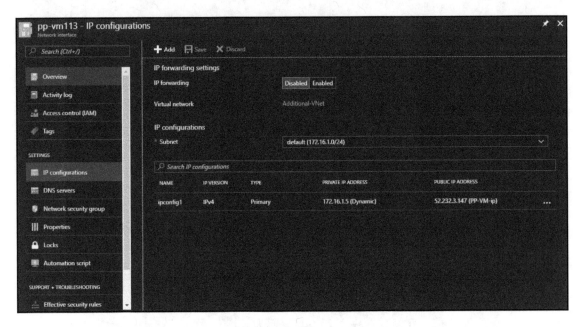

Figure 3.19: NIC blade overview

2. To enable **IP forwarding,** click on **Enabled** and then click **Save**. Enabling this feature will cause the NIC to receive traffic that is not destined to its own IP address. Traffic will be sent with a different source IP. This topic will be covered in further detail in the *User-defined routing* section in `Chapter 4`, *Network Connectivity Scenarios in Azure*.

3. To add another IP to the NIC, click on **Add**, and a new blade will pop up, for which you have to specify the following:
   - **Name**: The name of the IP.
   - **Type**: This field will be grayed out because a primary IP already exists. Therefore, this one will be secondary.
   - **Allocation**: Specify whether the allocation method is static or dynamic.

- **IP address**: Enter the static IP address that belongs to the same subnet that the NIC belongs to. If you have selected dynamic allocation, you cannot enter the IP address statically.
- **Public IP address**: Specify whether or not you need a public IP address for this IP configuration. If you do, you will be asked to configure the required settings.

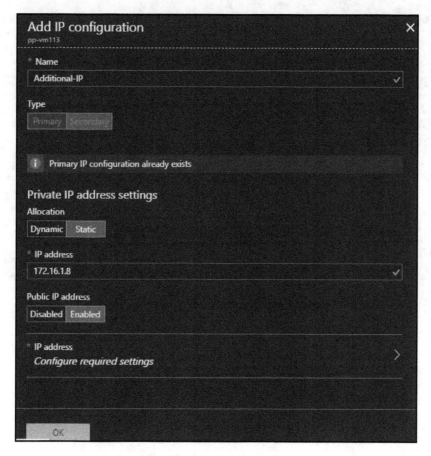

Figure 3.20: Configure the IP configuration settings

4. Click on **Configure required settings** for the public IP address and a
   new blade will pop up from which you can select an existing public IP
   address or create a new one, as shown in the following screenshot:

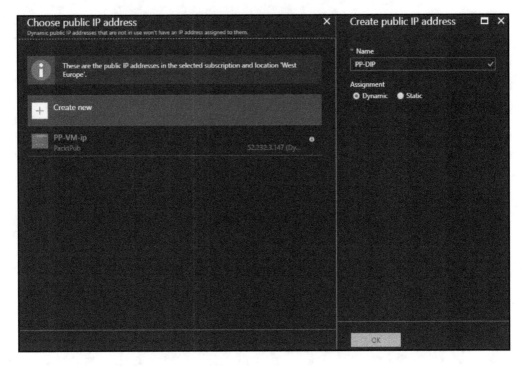

Figure 3.21: Create a new public IP address

5. **Click on OK** and you will return to the blade, as shown in *Figure 3.20*,
   with the following warning:

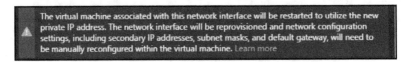

Figure 3.22: Warning for adding a new IP address

5. In this case, you need to plan for the addition of a new IP address to ensure that
   the time the VM is restarted is not during working hours.

Azure VNets considerations for Azure VMs

Building VMs in Azure is a common task, but to do this task well, and to make it operate properly, you need to understand the considerations of Azure VNets for Azure VMs. These considerations are as follows:

- Azure VNets enable you to bring your own IPv4/IPv6 addresses and assign them to Azure VMs, statically or dynamically
- You do not have access to the role that acts as DHCP or provides IP addresses; you can only control the ranges you want to use in the form of address ranges and subnets
- Installing a DHCP role on one of the Azure VMs is currently unsupported; this is because Azure does not use traditional Layer-2 or Layer-3 topology, and instead uses Layer-3 traffic with tunneling to emulate a Layer-2 LAN
- Private IP addresses can be used for internal communication; external communication can be done via public IP addresses
- You can assign multiple private and public IP addresses to a single VM
- You can assign multiple NICs to a single VM
- By default, all the VMs within the same virtual network can communicate with each other, unless otherwise specified by an NSG on a subnet within this virtual network
- The **network security group** (**NSG**) can sometimes cause an overhead; without this overhead, however, all VMs within the same subnet would communicate with each other
- By default, an inbound security rule is created for remote desktops for Windows-based VMs, and SSH for Linux-based VMs
- The inbound security rules are first applied on the NSG of the subnet and then the VM NIC NSG – for example, if the subnet's NSG allows HTTP traffic, it will pass through it; however, it may not reach its destination if the VM NIC NSG does not allow it
- The outbound security rules are applied for the VM NIC NSG first, and then applied on the subnet NSG
- Multiple NICs assigned to a VM can exist in different subnets
- Azure VMs with multiple NICs in the same availability set do not have to have the same number of NICs, but the VMs must have at least two NICs
- When you attach an NIC to a VM, you need to ensure that they exist in the same location and subscription

- The NIC and the VNet must exist in the same subscription and location
- The NIC's MAC address cannot be changed until the VM to which the NIC is assigned is deleted
- Once the VM is created, you cannot change the VNet to which it is assigned; however, you can change the subnet to which the VM is assigned
- You cannot attach an existing NIC to a VM during its creation, but you can add an existing NIC as an additional NIC
- By default, a dynamic public IP address is assigned to the VM during creation, but this address will change if the VM is stopped or deleted; to ensure it will not change, you need to ensure its IP address is static
- In a multi-NIC VM, the NSG that is applied to one NIC does not affect the others

Automating tasks

Let's automate the manual tasks that have been implemented so far.

Creating an Azure VM using Azure PowerShell

First, we need to retrieve the virtual network information and store it in a variable by running the following cmdlet:

```
$VNet = Get-AzureRmVirtualNetwork -Name PSVNet -ResourceGroupName PacktPub
```

The same also applies for the NSG, which is performed by running the following cmdlet:

```
$NSG = Get-AzureRmNetworkSecurityGroup -Name PSNSG -ResourceGroupName
PacktPub
```

Next, we need to create a public IP by running the following cmdlet:

```
$PIP = New-AzureRmPublicIpAddress -ResourceGroupName PacktPub -Location
WestEurope -AllocationMethod Dynamic -Name PacktPubVMPIP
```

After that, we have to create an NIC for the VM by running the following cmdlet:

```
$NIC = New-AzureRmNetworkInterface -ResourceGroupName PacktPub -Location
WestEurope -Name PacktPubVMNIC -SubnetId $VNet.Subnets[0].Id -
PublicIpAddressId $PIP.Id -NetworkSecurityGroupId $NSG.Id
```

Now we're done with the VM networking part. The next step is to specify the VM's settings and configurations by running the following cmdlet:

```
$VMConfig = New-AzureRmVMConfig -VMName PacktPubVMPS -VMSize Standard_D1_v2
| Set-AzureRmVMOperatingSystem -Windows -Credential (Get-Credential) -
ComputerName PackPubVMPS | Set-AzureRmVMSourceImage -PublisherName
MicrosoftWindowsServer -Offer WindowsServer -Skus 2016-Datacenter -Version
latest | Add-AzureRMVMNetworkInterface -Id $NIC.ID
```

You can get all the sizes of the VM at `Get-AzureRMVMSize -Location`, where you can also specify the location in which you are going to build your VM.

You will be prompted to enter the VM credentials when you run the preceding cmdlet.

Finally, to create the VM, you need to run the following cmdlet:

```
New-AzureRmVM -ResourceGroupName PacktPub -Location WestEurope -VM
$VMConfig
```

Creating an Azure VM using Azure CLI 2.0

Unlike Azure PowerShell, Azure VM creation in Azure CLI 2.0 can be done with only two commands.

The first command creates a storage account to store the VM data in; perform this with the following command:

```
Az storage account create --location westeurope --name packtpubsacli
--resource-group PacktPub --sku Standard_LRS
```

Now you can create the VM by running the following command:

```
az vm create --resource-group PacktPub --name PacktPubVMCLI --location
westeurope --size Standard_DS2 --image win2016datacenter --storage-account
packtpubsacli --use-unmanaged-disk --vnet-name PacktPubvNet
--vnet-addressprefix 192.168.0.0/16 --subnet S1 --subnet-address-prefix
192.168.1.0/24 --admin-username mwaly --admin-password P@cktPub@2018
```

Adding an inbound or outbound rule to an Azure VM using Azure PowerShell

To add an inbound or outbound security rule to an Azure VM means you have to add the rule to the NSG assigned to the NIC that was created earlier. Fortunately, doing that isn't difficult.

To add an inbound or outbound rule, you need to run the following cmdlet:

```
Add-AzureRmNetworkSecurityRuleConfig -NetworkSecurityGroup $NSG -Name HTTP-
Rule -Description "Allow HTTP" -Access Allow -Protocol Tcp
-Direction Inbound -Priority 1020 -SourceAddressPrefix *
-SourcePortRange * -DestinationAddressPrefix * -DestinationPortRange 80
```

After that, you have to save the preceding configuration by running the following cmdlet:

```
Set-AzureRmNetworkSecurityGroup -NetworkSecurityGroup $NSG
```

The difference between inbound and outbound rules is the `Direction` parameter, which depends on whether it has been specified as `Inbound` or `Outbound`.

Adding an inbound or outbound rule to an Azure VM using Azure CLI 2.0

The same process that we discussed earlier also applies here, although there is one difference: it can be done using the following single command:

```
az network nsg rule create --resource-group PacktPub --nsg-name CLINSG --
name allow-https --description "Allow access to port 80 for HTTP"
--access Allow --protocol Tcp --direction Inbound --priority 1030
--source-address-prefix "*" --source-port-range "*"
--destination-address-prefix "*" --destination-port-range "80"
```

Attaching an NIC to an Azure VM using Azure PowerShell

Since adding an NIC to an Azure VM requires the VM to be in a **Stopped (Deallocated)** state, you will have to run the following cmdlets:

```
$VM = Get-AzureRMVM -Name PacktPubVMPS -ResourceGroupName PacktPub
Stop-AzureRMVM -Name $VM -ResourceGroupName PacktPub
```

Next, you have to retrieve the subnet info to which the NIC will be assigned by running the following cmdlet:

```
$Subnet = Get-AzureRmVirtualNetworkSubnetConfig -Name NSubnet
-VirtualNetwork $VNet
```

After that, you can create the additional NIC by running the following cmdlet:

```
$AdditionalNIC = New-AzureRmNetworkInterface -ResourceGroupName PacktPub -
Name AddNICPS -Location WestEurope -SubnetId $Subnet.Id
```

You can also create the NIC using the same method discussed during the VM creation section earlier.

You're now done with NIC creation, but the NIC has not yet been added to the VM. To ensure that it is, you need to retrieve the NIC ID, which will be needed when you the NIC is added to the VM. Retrieve the ID by using the following cmdlet:

```
$NICId = (Get-AzureRmNetworkInterface -ResourceGroupName PacktPub -Name
AddNIC).Id
```

Now, you can add the NIC to the VM by running the following cmdlet:

```
Add-AzureRmVMNetworkInterface -VM $VM -Id $NICId | Update-AzureRmVm
-ResourceGroupName PacktPub
```

Voila! The new NIC has now been successfully added to the VM.

Now you can start the VM by running the following cmdlet:

```
Start-AzureRMVM -Name PacktPubVMPS -ResourceGroupName PacktPub
```

Attaching an NIC to an Azure VM using Azure CLI 2.0

First, you need to put the VM into a **Stopped (Deallocated)** state. You can do this by running the following command:

```
az vm deallocate --resource-group PacktPub --name PacktPubVMCLI
```

Next, you need to create an NIC by running the following command:

```
az network nic create --resource-group PacktPub --name AddNICCLI
--vnet-name CLIVNet --subnet S1 --network-security-group CLINSG
```

After that, you can add the NIC to the VM by running the following command:

```
az vm nic add --resource-group PacktPub --vm-name PacktPubVMCLI --nics
ADDNICCLI
```

Finally, you can start the VM by running the following command:

```
az vm start --resource-group PacktPub --name PacktPubVMCLI
```

Enabling IP forwarding using Azure PowerShell

Enabling IP forwarding using PowerShell has a gotcha, as you cannot enable it for an NIC by using the cmdlets we have already looked at.

Instead, you have to ensure that the NIC for which you want to enable IP forwarding is stored in a variable such as $NIC.

Then, you can run the following cmdlet:

```
$NIC.EnableIPForwarding = 1
```

Finally, you can save your configuration by running the following cmdlet:

```
$NIC | Set-AzureRmNetworkInterface
```

Enabling IP forwarding using Azure CLI 2.0

Unlike in PowerShell, in CLI 2.0, enabling IP forwarding is done by the following single command:

```
az network nic update --name ADDNICCLI --resource-group PacktPub --ip-
forwarding true
```

Adding an additional IP address using Azure PowerShell

Let's add additional private and public IP addresses to an NIC.

First, you need to create a public IP address by running the following cmdlet:

```
$PIP = New-AzureRmPublicIpAddress -Name NewPIP -ResourceGroupName PacktPub
-Location WestEurope -AllocationMethod Dynamic
```

Next, you add the desired public and private IP addresses with the following cmdlet:

```
New-AzureRmNetworkInterfaceIpConfig -Name AdditionalIPConfig-Subnet $Subnet
-PrivateIpAddress 192.168.1.10 -PublicIpAddress $PIP
```

Adding an additional IP address using Azure CLI 2.0

At the time of writing, there is no way to add additional private and public IP addresses to an NIC with IPs assigned to it, using Azure CLI.

Summary

In this chapter, we covered some of the most interesting elements about Azure VMs, as well as how can you configure them and design a better networking solution. As automation is becoming a time-saving requirement, we also looked at automating existing manual tasks, using Azure PowerShell and Azure CLI.

In the next chapter, we will look at network connectivity scenarios in Azure that will help you to customize your own networking solution.

Questions

- L-series is the best fit for video editing and graphics rendering scenarios: True or False?
- Only one public IP address can be assigned to an Azure VM: True or False?
- When you apply an NSG to a VM during VM creation, it is assigned automatically to all NICs added in the future: True or False?
- You can change the NIC MAC address once the VM to which it is attached is deleted: True or False?
- State and explain the three states of Azure VMs.
- In a nutshell, explain what you know about IP forwarding.
- Write a PowerShell script that creates a VM with two NICs assigned to it. Each NIC must have multiple private and public IP addresses with IP forwarding enabled.

Further information

You can check out the following links for more information about the topics covered in this chapter:

- Azure Storage: https://www.packtpub.com/big-data-and-business-intelligence/learning-microsoft-azure-storage
- VNets and VMs in Azure: https://docs.microsoft.com/en-us/azure/virtual-machines/windows/network-overview
- IP forwarding: https://docs.microsoft.com/en-us/azure/virtual-network/virtual-network-network-interface#enable-or-disable-ip-forwarding

4

Network Connectivity Scenarios in Azure

Introduction

In this chapter, different network connectivity scenarios will be introduced to you that will help with designing and implementing solutions that work on Azure, or span across Azure and your on-premises. This chapter will cover every scenario, accompanied with a step-by-step guide for **VNet-to-VNet** (**VNet2VNet**) connection, Point-to-Site connection, Site-to-Site connection, and user-defined routing. By the end of this chapter, you will be aware of how to design your network for many solutions, and even customize the network routes of Azure services.

Learning outcomes

The following topics will be covered:

- Introduction to network connectivity scenarios in Azure
- VNet2VNet connection
- Point-to-Site VPN connection
- Site-to-Site VPN connection
- ExpressRoute
- User-defined routing

Network connectivity scenarios in Azure

From what you have learned so far in Azure, you must know that Azure is a very flexible and customizable platform, and that applies to all its services, including networking services.

In a nutshell, the isolation that Azure provides to the virtual networks does not mean you cannot build your own routes to other virtual networks, or span your networking across on-premises and Azure.

Earlier, in `Chapter 2`, *Delving into Azure Virtual Networks*, you learned how to do VNet peering. Throughout this chapter, you will learn new and more ways to customize Azure networking, that includes, VNet2VNet connection, Point-to-Site connection, Site-to-Site connection, ExpressRoute, and user-defined routing.

In one sentence, when working in Azure, you can communicate with whatever you wish as the networking part will not be an obstacle.

VNet2VNet connection

As discussed in `Chapter 2`, *Delving into Azure Virtual Networks*, you can create a peer between two virtual networks within the same region to let the services within these two virtual networks communicate with each other seamlessly. At the time of writing you can peer two virtual networks within different regions, but this feature is still in preview, and not supported in all regions, and not even as highly available and reliable as the traditional peering. Therefore, we only have one way to do such a connection now: using VNet2VNet.

Creating a VNet2VNet connection is not similar to the model of VNet peering, because it uses a Site-to-Site IP Sec connection, which is similar to VPN communication with on-premises. Virtual network peering uses the Microsoft backbone network to communicate. As a result, when you want to deploy a VNet2VNet connection, you will need a VPN gateway to provide secure tunneling.

VNet2VNet connection benefits

We should learn why we would use such a feature, so the following points will illustrate why we use a VNet2VNet connection:

- Extending the virtual network communications to other regions, and subscriptions, which results in a well-connected, integrated environment for complicated applications.
- When using a VNet2VNet connection, you are using a VPN to enable the connection between them, which makes your connection more secure.
- When using virtual network peering across different subscriptions, you need to ensure that you have the required privilege for the other subscription. However, when using a VNet2VNet connection you do not have to, you only need some cooperation from the admin of the other subscription.

Creating a VNet2VNet connection

Creating a VNet2VNet connection is not a tough task. To create it, you need to perform the following steps:

1. Firstly, you need to create a virtual network gateway to act as a VPN device for each virtual network.
2. Search for `virtual network gateway`, as shown in the following screenshot:

Figure 4.1: Searching for virtual network gateways

3. Once clicked on **Virtual network gateways**, a new pane will be opened where you can view all the created virtual network gateways (if any), and create new virtual gateways, as shown in the following screenshot:

Figure 4.2: Virtual network gateways blade

4. To create a new virtual network gateway, click on **Add**, and a new blade will pop up in which you have to specify the following:
   - **Name**: Specify a name for the virtual network gateway.
   - **Gateway type**: There are two supported gateway types in Azure; **VPN** or **ExpressRoute**, and for the purpose of the current scenario VPN will be selected. (More information about ExpressRoute will be covered later in the chapter).
   - **VPN type**: Specify whether it will be **Route-based**, which uses dynamic routing, or **Policy-based**, which uses static routing. The route-based type will fit for almost every scenario.
   - **SKU**: Specify the SKU that would fit your scenario. Azure offers four VPN gateway SKUs, and every SKU has a different specification.
   - **Enable active-active mode**: If you selected any SKU other than the basic tier, you can enable this mode. If enabled, you will have to specify two gateway IP configurations with two public IP addresses.
   - **Virtual network**: Specify the virtual network for which you want to create a virtual network gateway.

- **First IP configuration**: Specify whether you want to create a new public IP address or you want to select an existing one that is not associated with other services.
- **Configure BGP ASN**: This option is available for route-based VPNs with SKUs other than basic, and it provides automatic and flexible network updates between different VNets.
- **Subscription**: Specify the subscription that will be charged for this service usage.
- **Location**: Specify the location at which this service will be built:

Figure 4.3: Creating a virtual network gateway

For more information about VPN gateway SKUs, you can check the following link: `https://docs.microsoft.com/en-us/azure/vpn-gateway/vpn-gateway-about-vpngateways#gwsku`. For more information about VPN gateway BGB, you can check the following link: `https://docs.microsoft.com/en-us/azure/vpn-gateway/vpn-gateway-bgp-overview`. For Test/Dev environments, you can use Basic SKU.

5. Then, you need to create another virtual network gateway, but this time it will be for the other virtual network.

6. Once you are done, you can navigate to one of the virtual network gateways you have created, and under **SETTINGS**, click on **Connections**, as shown in the following screenshot:

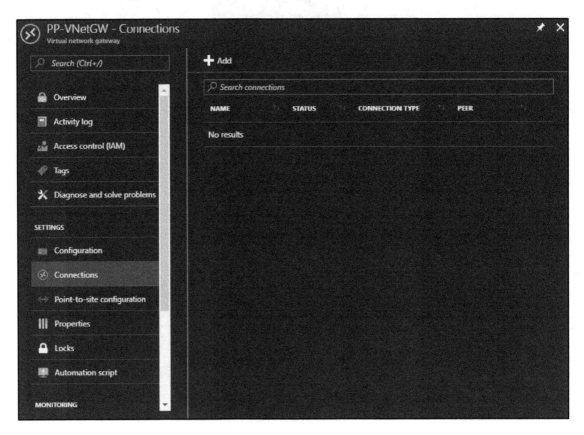

Figure 4.4: Virtual network gateway connections

7. Click on **Add**, and a new blade will pop up where you have to specify the
   following:
   - **Name**: The name of the connection.
   - **Connection type**: Select **VNet-to-VNet** for this scenario. There are two
     other types that will be discussed later.
   - **First virtual network gateway**: This connection is added by default for
     the virtual network gateway on which you have opened the
     Connections blade.
   - **Second virtual network gateway**: Specify the other virtual network
     gateway.
   - **Shared key (PSK)**: A mixture of letters and numbers used to establish
     the connection between the two virtual network gateways. It is
     recommended that you make it as complex as possible, but keep a copy
     of it as it will be needed later:

Figure 4.5: Configuring a VNet2VNet connection

8. You have to do the same thing on the other virtual network connection. As a result, the connection will be successfully established between the two VNets, and the status of the connections will be **Connected**, as shown in the following screenshot:

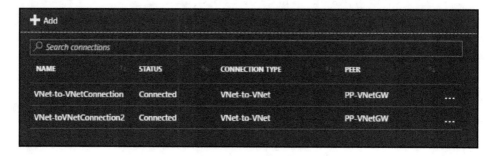

Figure 4.6: The connection has been successfully established between the two VNets

VNet2VNet connection key points

The following key points are recommended to be considered when working with VNet2VNet connections:

- Communications between VNets is not high, as it is constrained by the VPN gateway speed
- Ensure that there are no IPs overlapping between the two VNets
- To avoid unexpected functioning of VPN gateways, avoid associating NSGs to gateway subnets
- Traffic between VNets in different regions is charged for the outbound traffic
- Traffic flows between VNets via the Microsoft Azure backbone network
- IPsec/IKE encryption is used to protect the VNet2VNet connection
- A VNet2VNet connection between public Azure VNets, and German, US Government, and Chinese Azure VNets cannot be created
- A VNet with a route-based VPN type cannot be connected to a VNet with a policy-based VPN type
- As discussed earlier, you need to create a virtual network gateway for each VNet you want to add to a VNet2VNet connection, which will incur more charges
- A gateway subnet is required for each VNet you want to build a virtual network gateway for
- VMs cannot be deployed to a gateway subnet

- Static public IP address allocation for a VPN gateway is not allowed
- Policy-based VPN is not supported for a VNet2VNet connection

Point-to-Site connection

Securing communication between you and the Azure services is a very important matter. That is why it might seem cool to connect to Azure via a VPN tunnel instead of the public internet. Therefore, you can connect to your Azure VMs as they exist in the local network whenever needed, if you do not prefer to do a Site-to-Site VPN connection and you only want specific clients to connect to Azure that way.

Point-to-Site connection advantages

A Point-to-Site connection has the following advantages:

- Helps you to create a secure connection from one client to a specific virtual network
- Supports Windows and macOS devices
- It does not need to have a VPN device, or even a public IP address, as it creates the VPN connection over SSTP or IKEv2 protocols

Creating a Point-to-Site connection

To create a Point-to-Site connection, you have to perform the following steps:

1. Ensure you have a virtual network with a gateway subnet, but avoid IPs overlapping with your on-premises.
2. Build a virtual network gateway for the virtual network you've created.
3. Then, you need to generate a certificate to allow a client to authenticate the VNet over a Point-to-Site VPN connection. This can be done either by a CA server or self-signed certificate.
4. To create a self-signed certificate, you can run the following PowerShell cmdlet:

```
$cert = New-SelfSignedCertificate -Type Custom -KeySpec Signature -
Subject "CN=RootCert" -KeyExportPolicy Exportable -HashAlgorithm
sha256 -KeyLength 2048 -CertStoreLocation "Cert:\CurrentUser\My" -
KeyUsageProperty Sign -KeyUsage CertSign
```

5. Then, open **Manage user certificates** and navigate to **Current User** | **Personal** | **Certificates** where you can find the certificate you have just created, as shown in the following screenshot:

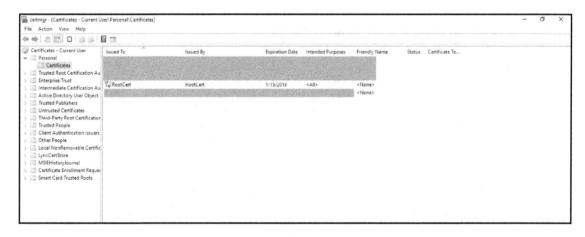

Figure 4.7: Root cert location

6. Right-click on the certificate you have created, then select **All Tasks** | **Export...**, as shown in the following screenshot:

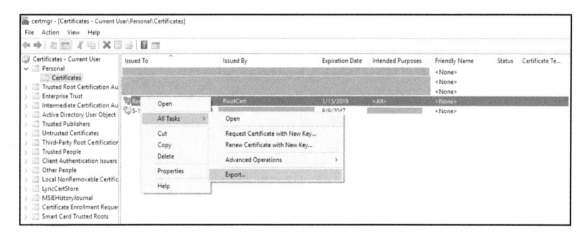

Figure 4.8: Exporting the certificate

7. You will be prompted by a welcome screen. Click on **Next**.

8. Then, select not to export the private key and click on **Next**, as shown in the following screenshot:

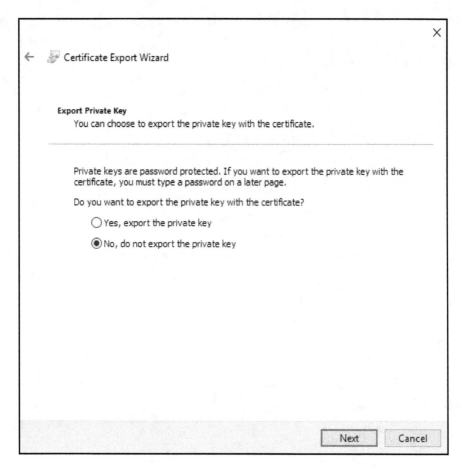

Figure 4.9: Determining whether to export the private key or not

9. After that, you have to specify the certificate format and **Base-64 encoded X.509 (.CER)** will be selected, as shown in the following screenshot:

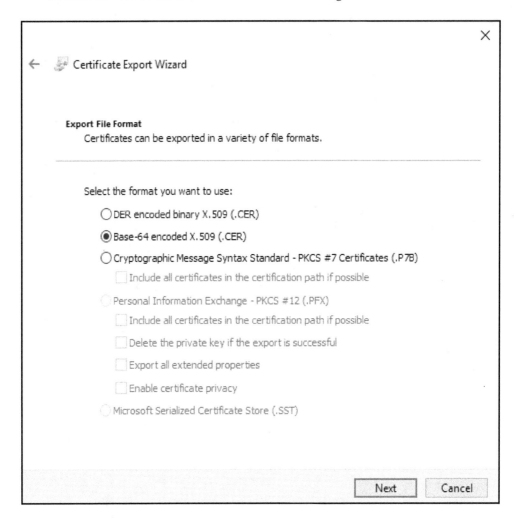

Figure 4.10: Select the file format of the certificate

10. On the next screen, you have to specify the path to where the certificate will be exported, as shown in the following screenshot:

Figure 4.11: Export file path

11. Finally, you will be presented with a summary of all the settings you have specified during the export process, as shown in the following screenshot:

Figure 4.12: Certificate export summary

12. After clicking on **Finish**, a wizard will pop up confirming that the export was successful, as shown in the following screenshot:

Figure 4.13: Successful export

13. Navigate to where the certificate has been exported and open it with Notepad. Copy the certificate data, as shown in the following screenshot:

Figure 4.14: Copying the certificate data

14. Navigate back to the virtual network gateway you have created on the Azure portal, and open **Point-to-site configuration**, as shown in the following screenshot:

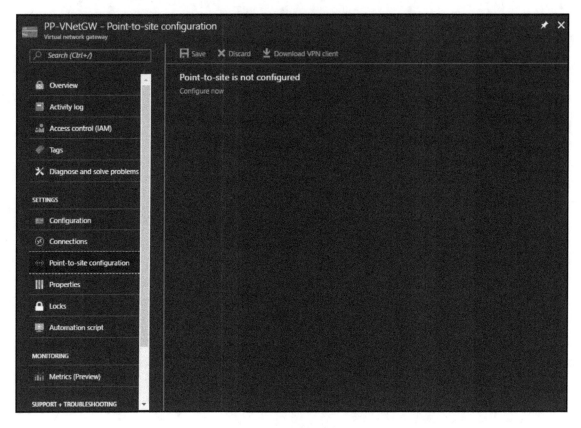

Figure 4.15: Point-to-Site configuration blade

15. Click on **Configure now**, and the following fields will appear in the same blade:
    - **Address pool**: The IP address range of your environment.
    - **Tunnel type**: Select the tunnel type that will fit the client/s that will connect to the VNet over the Point-to-Site VPN connection.
    - **Authentication type**: There are two authentication types—**Azure certificate** and **RADIUS authentication**, which is still in preview at the time of writing. Select **Azure certificate** as it will fit this scenario.

- **Root certificates**: Specify a name for the certificates and paste the data you copied earlier under public certificate data.
- **Revoked certificates**: You can revoke specific client certificates by entering a name for the certificate and its thumbprint:

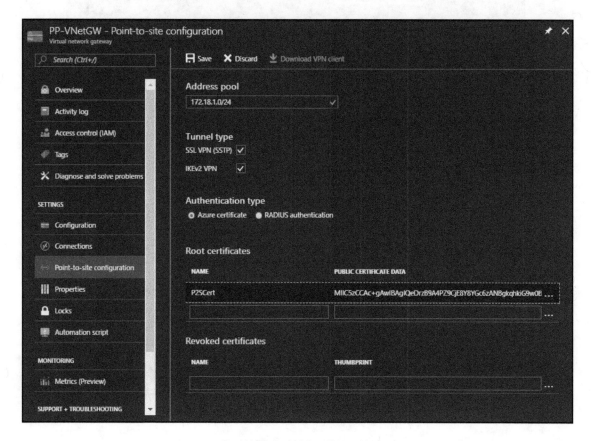

Figure 4.16: Configuring Point-to-Site connection

16. Click on **Save**, and it will take a while to save the configuration. You will be able to **Download VPN client**, as shown in the following screenshot:

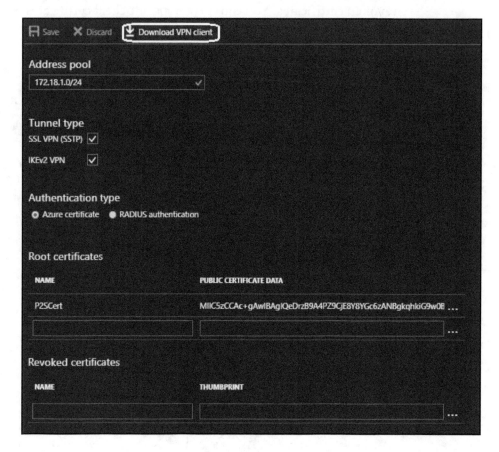

Figure 4.17: Download VPN client

17. A zipped file will be downloaded. Unzip the file and three folders will be generated:
    - `Generic`: Contains general information about the VPN client configuration that was specified earlier, and a certificate that needs to be installed
    - `WindowsAmd64`: Contains the executable for all 64-bit Windows clients
    - `WindowsX86`: Contains the executable for all 32-bit Windows clients

18. Install the certificate in the `Generic` folder, all you need to do is accept its defaults.

19. Install the executable that will fit your OS.

20. Once it is installed, you will note that a VPN connection has been added to your connections, as shown in the following screenshot:

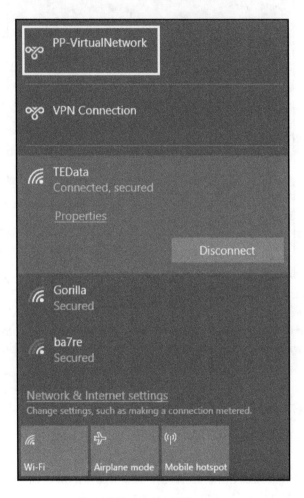

Figure 4.18: The networks and VPN connections

21. Click on the VPN connection, **PP-VirtualNetwork**, and click on **Connect**, as shown in the following screenshot:

Figure 4.19: Connect to the VNet

22. Now, you can use a remote desktop to log on to any VM that exists within the virtual network you are connected to remotely, using its private IP address.

Point-to-Site connection key points

The following key points are important for a better understanding of Point-to-Site connections:

- A Point-to-Site VPN connection can only work with a virtual network gateway and a route-based VPN type
- To connect from Mac devices, you need to make sure that IKEv2 VPN is selected as a tunnel type during the Point-to-Site configuration
- Only one address pool for the network you are connecting from can be added
- You cannot upload more than 20 root certificates for a Point-to-Site connection

Site-to-Site connection

Lately, I have been working with many customers who are embracing Azure and its services. Therefore, I've been working on many projects where customers want to build a disaster recovery site on Azure, migrate some of their workloads to Azure, or even build some Azure VMs that can work side by side with their on-premises environment. All of these scenarios are achievable but only with the help of a Site-to-Site VPN connection, which will link Azure with on-premises. In other words, you cannot extend your on-premises to Azure without understanding Site-to-Site VPN connection.

Site-to-Site connection benefits

There are many benefits of using a Site-to-Site connection. Here are some of them:

- Extend your on-premises to the cloud securely
- On-ramp for migrating services to the cloud
- Use your on-premises resources in Azure and vice versa

Creating a Site-to-Site connection

Creating a Site-to-Site VPN connection is not a very straightforward process, as you need to get your hands dirty on both sides (Azure and on-premises). However, I'll do my best to simplify the process. Since it needs some configuration on both sides, you may wonder what exactly needs to be done on both sides. Actually, it will need a VPN device in your on-premises to act as a gateway for your environment through which the traffic will go to an Azure gateway, and then to Azure virtual networks.

So, before getting our hands dirty with configuring the Site-to-Site VPN connection, you need to consider the following points before getting started:

- Make sure that your VPN device is supported to work with the Azure virtual network gateway without any problems. See the following link: `https://docs.microsoft.com/en-us/azure/vpn-gateway/vpn-gateway-about-vpn-devices#known`.
- Check how to do the configuration to your gateway at the following link: `https://docs.microsoft.com/en-us/azure/vpn-gateway/vpn-gateway-3rdparty-device-config-overview`.

- If you are not using any supported VPN devices, you can use **Routing and Remote Access Service (RRAS)** as your local VPN, which will be used in our scenario.
- Plan the address spaces and subnets for the virtual networks you will be using in Azure, in a manner that does not cause any IP address overlapping between Azure virtual networks and your on-premises.

Without further ado, let's get our hands dirty with configuring a Site-to-Site VPN connection:

1. First off, make sure you have an available VM or a physical server that can be used to act as a local VPN by installing RRAS on it.
2. Make sure the VM/physical server has two NICs, one of them will be used for internal communication with an IP address assigned to it, and the other one will be used for communication with the Azure virtual network gateway with a public IP address assigned to it.
      - The NIC that will be used for internal communication must not have a gateway IP address assigned to it, to ensure that the traffic is routed via the NIC with the public IP address.
      - Uncheck all the properties of the NIC with a public IP address except TCP/IPv4, as it will be used to statically enter the IP address.
      - Disable IPv6 for both NICs by unchecking it in the NIC properties.
      - Disable NetBIOS over TCP. You can do so by navigating to TCP/IPv4 properties **Advanced | WINS** and disable NetBIOS over TCP/IP.
3. Now, you can install RRAS, but make sure to select the **DirectAccess and VPN (RAS)** role service during the installation.
4. Navigate back to the Azure portal and create a virtual network with the address spaces and subnets according to what you have planned, and don't forget about the gateway subnet that will be used for the virtual network gateway.
5. Then, create a virtual network gateway and assign the virtual network you created earlier to it.
6. Then, search for `local network gateway`, which will be used to connect your local network with Azure networks, as shown in the following screenshot:

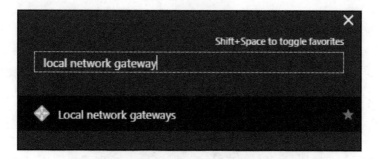

Figure 4.20: Searching for local network gateways

7. Once its blade is opened, all the created local network gateways will be displayed, as shown in the following screenshot:

Figure 4.21: Local network gateways blade

8. Click on **Add**, and a new blade will pop up where you have to specify the following:
    - **Name**: The name of the local network gateway
    - **IP address**: The public IP address of the RRAS server (local VPN)
    - **Address space**: Add the address space of your local network
    - **Subscription**: Specify the subscription that will be charged for this service
    - **Resource group**: Specify the resource group in which the local network gateway will exist

- **Location**: The location of the local network gateway:

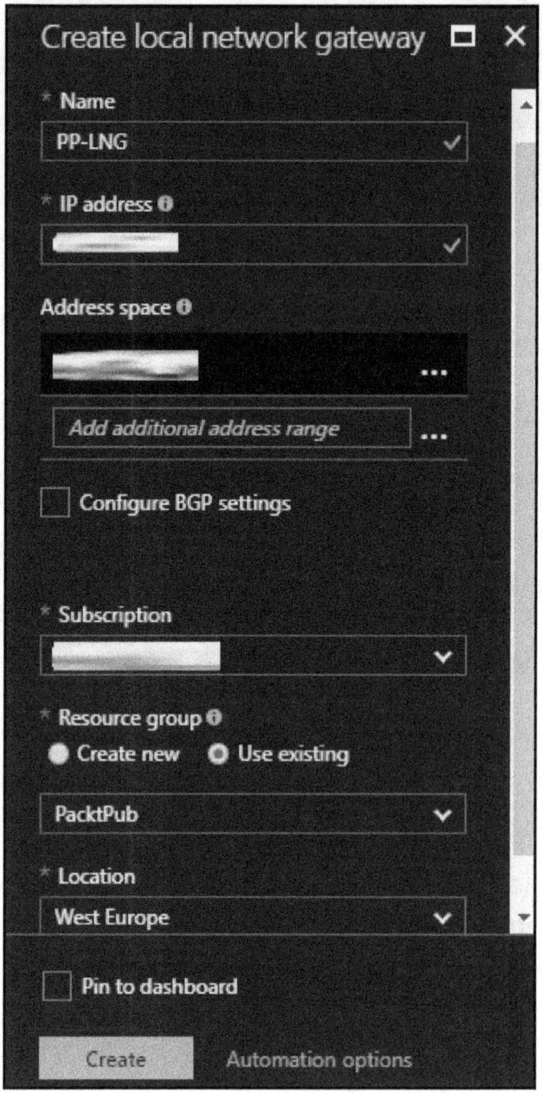

Figure 4.22: Configure the local network gateway

9. Click on **Create**, and wait until the local network gateway is created.
10. Navigate to the created virtual network gateway then click on **Connections**, as shown in the following screenshot:

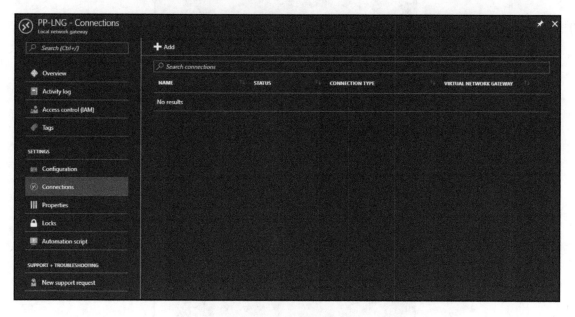

Figure 4.23: Local network gateway connections

11. Click on **Add**, and a new blade will pop up where you have to specify the following:
      - **Name**: The name of the connection
      - **Virtual network gateway**: Specify the virtual network gateway that you have created for that purpose

- **Shared key (PSK)**: Specify a shared key, which will be used to initiate the connections from on-premises:

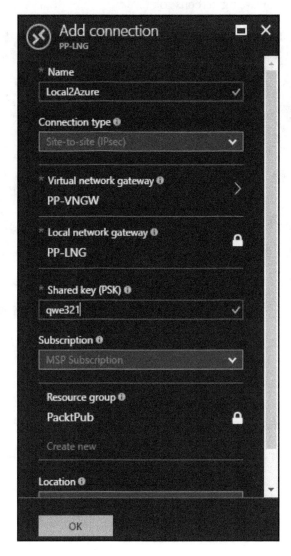

Figure 4.24: Adding a connection between the local network gateway and virtual network gateway

12. Click on **OK**, and the connection will be added.

13. Once the connection is added, navigate back to the RRAS server and open the **Routing and Remote Access** console, as shown in the following screenshot:

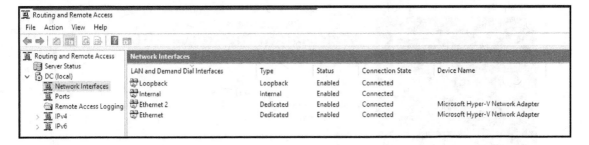

Figure 4.25: Routing and Remote Access console

14. Right-click on **Network Interfaces** and click on **New Demand-dial Interface...**, as shown in the following screenshot:

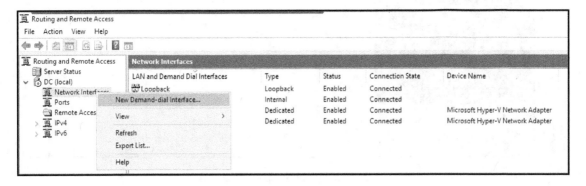

Figure 4.26: Create New Demand-dial Interface

15. A new wizard will appear with a welcome screen, so click on **Next**, as shown in the following screenshot:

Figure 4.27: Welcome screen for creating demand-dial interface

16. On the next screen, you have to specify a name for the interface, as shown in the following screenshot:

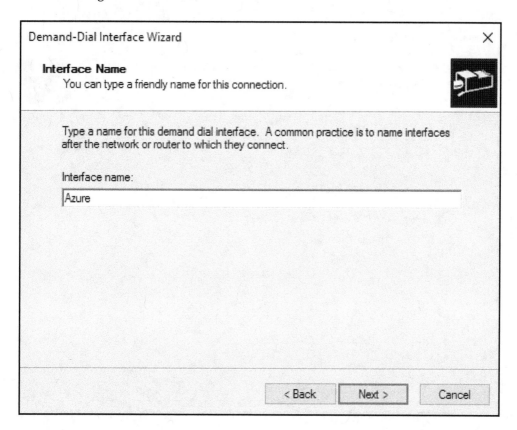

Figure 4.28: Specify an interface name

17. On the next screen, you have to specify the **Connection Type**, which would be VPN in our scenario, as shown in the following screenshot:

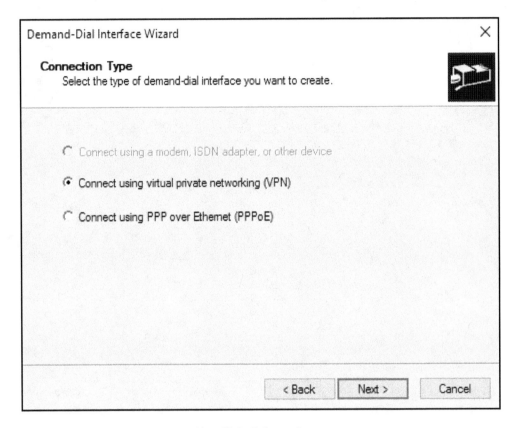

Figure 4.29: Specify the connection type

18. On the next screen, you have to select the **VPN Type**, which would be **IKEv2** in our scenario, as shown in the following screenshot:

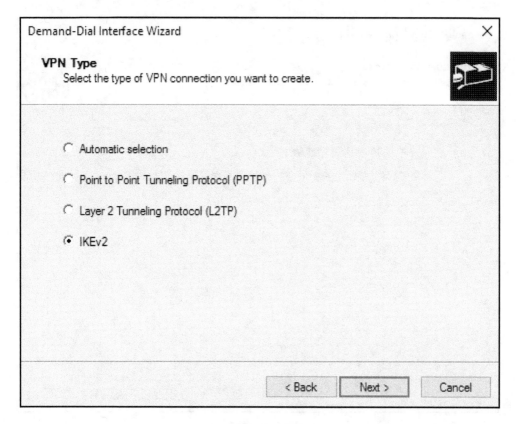

Figure 4.30: Specify the VPN type

19. On the next screen, you have to enter the public IP address of the virtual network gateway. You can get it from the overview of the virtual network gateway from the Azure portal.

20. On the next screen, you can select transports and security options for this connection, which will be left at the default, as shown in the following screenshot:

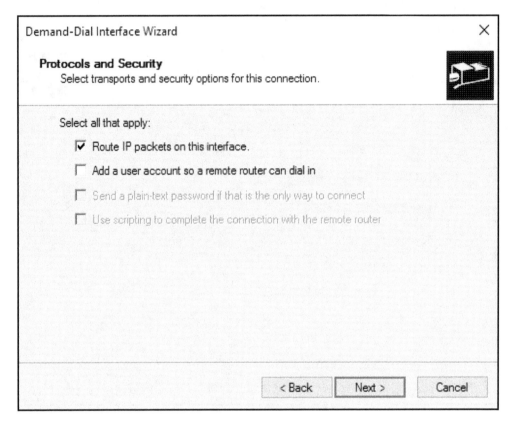

Figure 4.31: Select transports and security options for the connection

21. On the next screen, you have to create a static route to all the address spaces of the virtual network by adding them, as shown in the following screenshot:

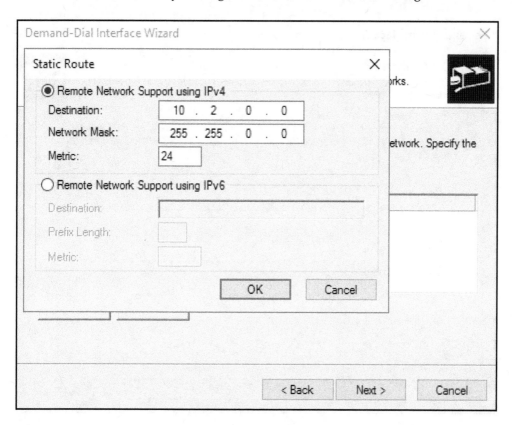

Figure 4.32: Create a static route to Azure virtual network address spaces

22. On the next screen, you can specify the dial-out credentials but it's okay if you want to enter the **User name** only, as shown in the following screenshot:

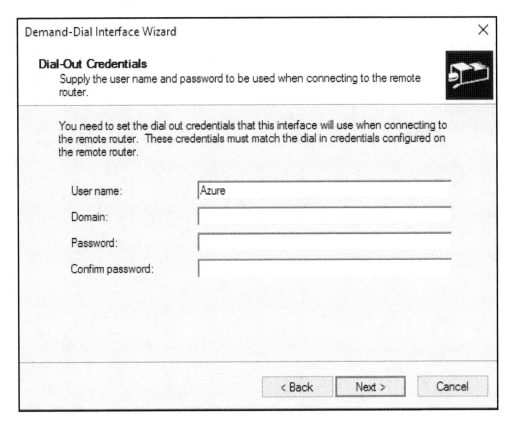

Figure 4.33: Specify the dial-out credentials

23. Finally, all you need to do is click on **Finish**, as shown in the following screenshot:

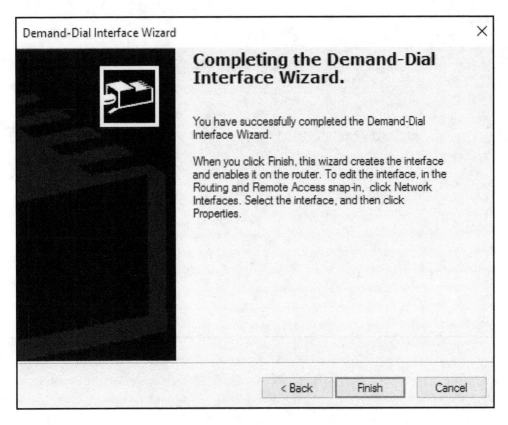

Figure 4.34: Finishing the demand-dial interface creation

24. Once the interface is created, right-click on it and select **Properties**, as shown in the following screenshot:

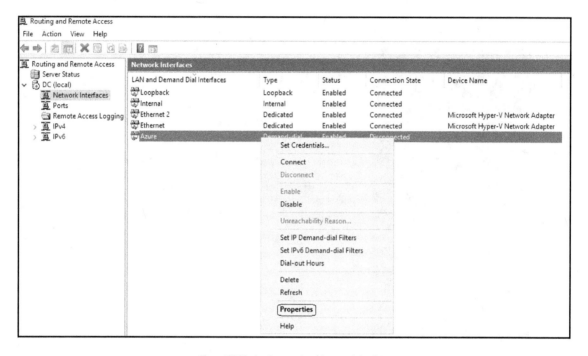

Figure 4.35: Viewing the properties of the network interface

25. Navigate to the **Security** tab. Under **Authentication**, **Use preshared key for authentication** will be selected, and the shared key that was entered earlier when creating the connection between the local network gateway and the virtual network gateway will be entered, as shown in the following screenshot:

Figure 3.36: Setting the authentication type

26. Click **OK**, right-click on the network interface, and select **Connect** to initiate the connection between your environment and Azure, as shown in the following screenshot:

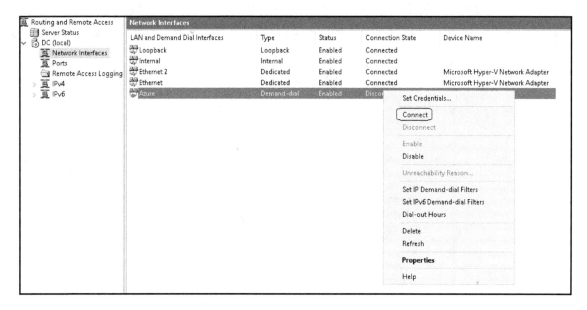

Figure 4.37: Initiate the connection between Azure and the local network

27. Now, you can connect to any VM located on the virtual network you have built in Azure by its private IP address.

Site-to-Site connection key points

The following key points are important for a better understanding of Site-to-Site connections:

- For policy-based VPN gateways, when the VPN traffic is idle for more than five minutes, the VPN tunnel goes down
- Most of the software VPN solutions should work with Azure gateway as long as they conform to industry standard IPSec implementations
- Site-to-Site and Point-to-Site configurations can coexist in the same virtual network

ExpressRoute

Extending your on-premises network to Azure is not constrained by initiating a VPN connection to Azure. Microsoft provides another method called ExpressRoute, using which you can create a private connection between your on-premises and Microsoft data centers. Unlike VPN connections, it does not create VPN tunnels over the internet to reach Azure services, as it is directly connected to Microsoft data centers.

By following this model, you can have a faster, more reliable, higher-security, lower-latency connection than the other options.

At present, ExpressRoute is supported in all Azure regions. However, you need to have an ExpressRoute national cloud peering that will act as the connectivity provider between your on-premises and Azure. Unfortunately, not all the countries have ExpressRoute national cloud peering, which means some countries do not benefit from this feature.

 For more information about ExpressRoute partners and peering locations, check the following link: `https://docs.microsoft.com/en-us/azure/expressroute/expressroute-locations`.

ExpressRoute benefits

The following points are the benefits of ExpressRoute:

- A reliable connection to Azure services with a high-speed connection and low latency
- Dynamic routing is provided between your on-premises and Microsoft data centers using BGP
- Different connectivity models are supported, which will be discussed further in the chapter
- Connectivity to all Microsoft services, such as Microsoft Azure, Office 365, and Dynamics 365
- Predictable performance and lower cost

ExpressRoute connectivity models

At present, there are three connectivity models:

- Co-location at a cloud exchange
- Point-to-Point Ethernet connection
- Any-to-any (IPVPN) connection

Co-location at a cloud exchange

When using such a model, you can get your infrastructure co-located in a facility with a cloud exchange. Such a model would enable you to have a virtual cross connection to the Microsoft cloud via the provider's Ethernet exchange.

That model would offer either Layer 2 cross connections, and you take care of the Layer 3 connections, or managed Layer 3 connections between your infrastructure and the Microsoft cloud.

Point-to-Point Ethernet connection

Unlike the previous model, in this one you will have your infrastructure in your own data centers and initiate Point-to-Point Ethernet links. However, there's a similarity in the connection method, as it offers either Layer 2 connections or managed Layer 3 connections between your on-premises environment and the Microsoft cloud.

Any-to-any (IPVPN) connection

This model will integrate your WAN with the Microsoft cloud. This model provides a connection between your branch offices and data centers using MPLS, and the same is done when connecting to Azure. As a result, everything is virtually, directly connected to everything. In other words, if you want to communicate with the Microsoft cloud from a branch office, the communication process does not have to go through your data centers, however it can communicate with the Microsoft cloud directly.

User-defined routes

As you have noticed, most of our work is done without the need to do routing manually, because Azure does that part for us, and creates default system routes in an Azure route table to allow the following:

- Traffic within the VNet
- Traffic between different VNets connected via the Azure VPN gateway
- Traffic between the VNet and the internet
- Traffic between the virtual network and other networks connected via Azure VPN gateway

So, you might wonder, *can I do some customization other than the default system routes?*

The answer is *Absolutely, yes.*

You can create your own routes between the networks to fulfill your scenarios.

Creating a user-defined route

Creating a user-defined route is not a complicated process, all you need to do is perform the following steps:

1. Search for `route tables`, and open its blade.

2. Click on **Add** to create your customized route, as shown in the following screenshot:

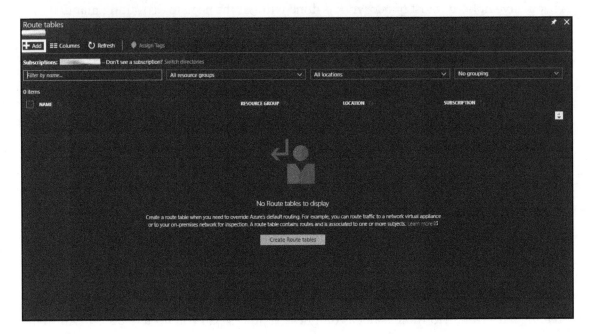

Figure 4.38: Route tables blade

3. A new blade will pop up, wherein you have to fill in the following:
    - **Name**: A name for the route
    - **Subscription**: Specify the subscription that will be charged for using this service
    - **Resource group**: The resource group within which the route table will exist
    - **Location**: The location where this service will be built:

Figure 4.39: Create a new route table

4. Once you have clicked on **Create**, the route table will be created.
5. Navigate to the created route table, as shown in the following screenshot:

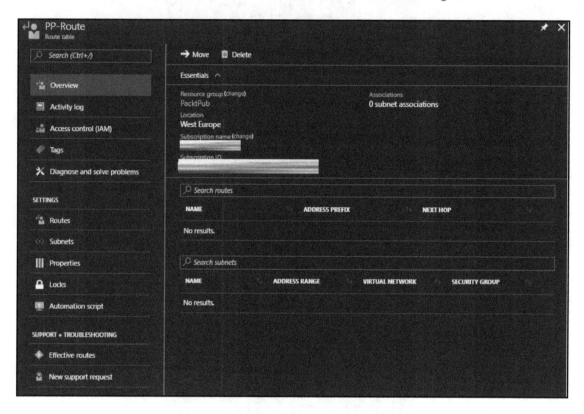

Figure 4.40: Route table overview

6. Navigate to **Routes**, under **SETTINGS**, as shown in the following screenshot:

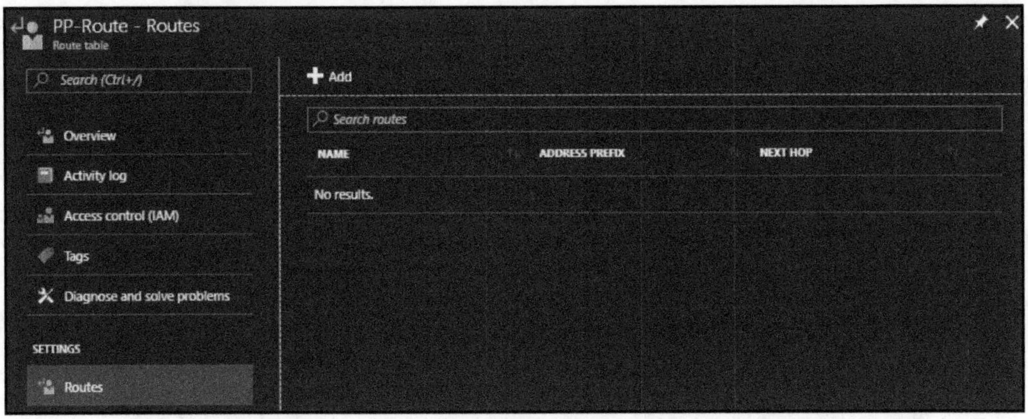

Figure 4.41: Routes

7. Click on **Add**, and a new blade will be opened, asking you to specify the following:

    - **Route name**: A name for the route.
    - **Address prefix**: The destination IP address range in CIDR notation that this route applies to. If the destination address of a packet falls in this range, it matches this route.
    - **Next hop type**: The next hop handles the matching packets for this route. It can be one of the following:
        - **Virtual Network: Traffic between different address ranges within an address spaces in a virtual network can be routed by selecting this type.**
        - **Virtual Network Gateway: This type would be used when you have a site-to-site VPN connection and you want to customize the routes between your on-premises and Azure.**
        - **Internet:** This type of hops can be used when you want to customize the routes to the internet.
        - **Virtual Appliance:** In case you have a virtual appliance which you are using to route traffic, you can select it as the next hop type and once the traffic get to the virtual appliance, it would take care of the routing process.
        - **None:** This type would drop the traffic whenever it goes out from the subnet this route will be attached to.

- **Next hop address**: The IP address of the next hop. This can only be set when the next hop type is **Virtual appliance**:

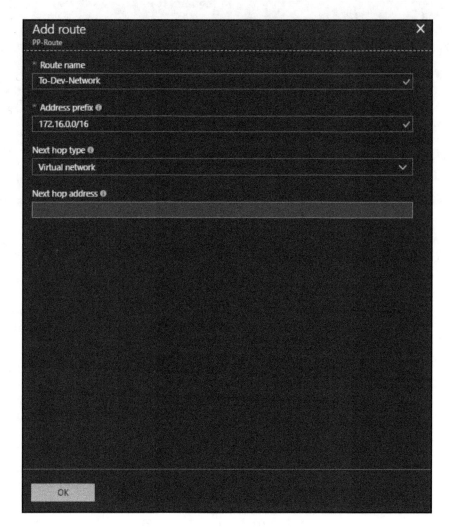

Figure 4.42: Create a new route

8. Once, the route is created, navigate to **Subnets**, which is located after **Routes**, as shown in the following screenshot:

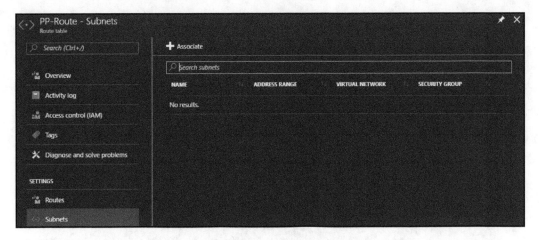

Figure 4.43: The subnets to which the route is assigned blade

9. Click on **Associate** to specify the subnet that will use this customized route to reach the virtual network specified during the route creation.

10. First off, specify the **Virtual network** within which the subnet exists, as shown in the following screenshot:

Figure 4.44: Specify the virtual network within which the subnet exists

11. Then, specify the **Subnet**, as shown in the following screenshot:

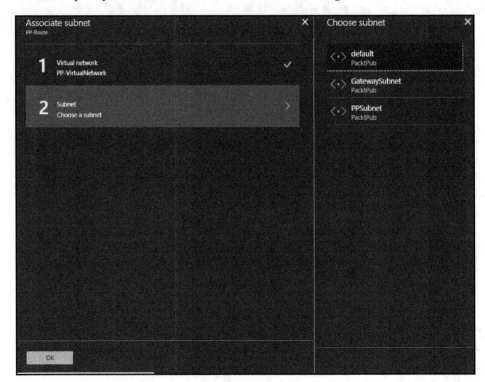

Figure 4.45: Specify the subnet that will be associated to the route

12. Then, click on **OK** and the subnet will be associated. As a result, any VM with an IP address in the range of this subnet can reach out to any VM with an IP address in the virtual network specified in the route.

User-defined routing key points

The following key points should be considered for a better understanding of user-defined routing:

- If the next hop type you have specified is a **Virtual appliance**, you must enable IP forwarding for the VM of the virtual appliance.

- User-defined routing can be used for forced tunneling in Site-to-Site VPN scenarios. For example, if you want all the internet traffic of Azure VMs to get redirected back to your on-premises for auditing and inspection.
- NSG is a very basic firewall that does not provide filtering, inspection, and so on, therefore you can use user-defined routing with a virtual appliance that will provide the new era security requirements when it comes to this part.
- You can find many network virtual appliances from many brands, such as Cisco, Fortinet, Citrix, Paloalto, F5, and so on, in the Azure Marketplace.

Summary

This chapter has covered some of the most important network connectivity scenarios that are implemented in almost every environment. If you cannot find a VNet2VNet connection suitable for your scenario, you will find the Point-to-Site connection, Site-to-Site connection, or even user-defined routing fits. In a nutshell, you will definitely need one of these scenarios for your environment.

Questions

- VNet2VNet connection cannot be used to connect virtual networks from different subscriptions (true/false)
- The routes you create in the route table can only be associated to subnets (true/false)
- VPN Gateway is not a requirement for implementing a VNet2VNet connection (true/false)
- What is the difference between route-based and policy-based VPN types?
- State the supported authentication types for a Point-to-Site VPN connection
- State and explain the ExpressRoute connectivity models
- How long does it take for the VPN tunnel to go down for policy based VPN gateways when the VPN traffic is idle?

Further information

If you are interested in learning more about the topics that have been covered, you can check the following links:

- **Planning and design for VPN gateway**: `https://docs.microsoft.com/en-us/azure/vpn-gateway/vpn-gateway-plan-design`
- **Overview of BGP with Azure VPN gateways**: `https://docs.microsoft.com/en-us/azure/vpn-gateway/vpn-gateway-bgp-overview`
- **Highly available cross-premises and VNet2VNet connectivity**: `https://docs.microsoft.com/en-us/azure/vpn-gateway/vpn-gateway-highlyavailable`
- **About Point-to-Site VPN**: `https://docs.microsoft.com/en-us/azure/vpn-gateway/point-to-site-about`
- **Configure Point-to-Site connections—RADIUS authentication**: `https://docs.microsoft.com/en-us/azure/vpn-gateway/point-to-site-how-to-radius-ps`
- **Connect virtual networks from different deployment models**: `https://docs.microsoft.com/en-us/azure/vpn-gateway/vpn-gateway-connect-different-deployment-models-portal`
- **ExpressRoute prerequisites and checklist**: `https://docs.microsoft.com/en-us/azure/expressroute/expressroute-prerequisites`
- **ExpressRoute workflows for circuit provisioning and circuit states**: `https://docs.microsoft.com/en-us/azure/expressroute/expressroute-workflows`
- **ExpressRoute routing requirements**: `https://docs.microsoft.com/en-us/azure/expressroute/expressroute-routing`

5

Azure DNS

Introduction

In this chapter, you will be introduced to Azure DNS and how to work with it. That includes managing Azure DNS zones and records. Moreover, Azure DNS delegation will be covered, and even Azure reverse DNS. We will also talk about private DNS zones, which is a new feature that will add more customization to your solution. Finally, you will learn how to automate all the tasks that have been manually done throughout the chapter.

Learning outcomes

The following topics will be covered:

- Introduction to Azure DNS
- Azure DNS zones and records
- Azure DNS delegation
- Azure reverse DNS zone
- Private Azure DNS zones
- Automate the tasks

Azure DNS

DNS, which stands for **Domain Name System**, is one of the most important services that has been used for a long time. In a nutshell, it does translate the service names, for example, a website to an IP address. Azure provides DNS as a service by which you can host your domains in Azure, which will provide name translation using Microsoft Azure infrastructure with 99.99% availability SLA. At the time of writing, it does not support domain name purchasing.

> In May 2015, Microsoft announced the public preview of Azure DNS at the Ignite conference. After that, the service was used by many customers who delivered great feedback that made the service more mature, and in September 2016 Microsoft announced the general availability of Azure DNS.

Azure DNS benefits

Using Azure DNS will provide you with the following benefits:

- **Speedy**: By using Azure DNS, you are using one of the generally available Azure services, which is hosted on all Azure regions. As a result, anyone who tries to translate a specific service name to an IP address will be using the nearest Azure region to them, which will provide better performance for customers across the world, because Microsoft's name severs use any cast networking, so all the DNS queries are routed to the nearest server.
- **High availability**: Azure DNS is scalable and redundant across all Azure regions. As a result, it is resilient to failures even if a complete region faces a disaster.
- **Security**: Like every service in Azure, Azure DNS is secured with many things, such as **Role-Based Access Control (RBAC)**, multi-factor authentication, resource locking, and so on.
- **Easier management**: You can manage all your DNS zones and records from one interface, either by the Azure portal, Azure PowerShell, Azure CLI, and so on. As a result, it will be more convenient to manage Azure services and their DNS from one place.
- **Supportability of common DNS records**: Almost all the common DNS record types are supported by Azure DNS, such as A, AAAA, CNAME, PTR, SOA, SRV, MX, NS, and TXT.

- **Simple migration**: The process of migrating your domain hosting to Azure DNS is very quick and simple.
- **Third-party support**: Azure DNS can be managed by third-party tools, such as Men & Mice.

Azure DNS zones and records

A DNS zone is like a container for the records for a specific domain, and the zone is named according to the domain. For example, the domain name is watermelon.com and the zone name will be the same, whereas the records represent something within that domain. For example, you would create a record named www for the company website, which will be formatted as Record.DomainName. Therefore, in our scenario, it would look as follows: www.watermelon.com.

Without further ado, let's dive deep into creating a DNS zone and a record.

Creating a DNS zone

Creating a DNS zone is not a tough process. Just perform the following steps:

1. On Azure portal, search for DNS zones, as shown in the following screenshot:

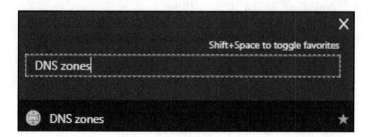

Figure 5.1: Searching for DNS zones

2. Click on it, and a new blade will be opened from which you will create a new DNS zone by clicking on **Add**, as shown in the following screenshot:

Figure 5.2: DNS zones blade

3. A new blade will pop up, wherein you have to specify the following:
    - **Name**: A name for the zone.
    - **Subscription**: The subscription that will be charged for using this service.
    - **Resource group**: The resource group within which this service will exist.
    - **Resource group location**: If you select to create a new resource group, you can specify in which region you will create this resource group. Consider that DNS zone service is global and not bound to location.

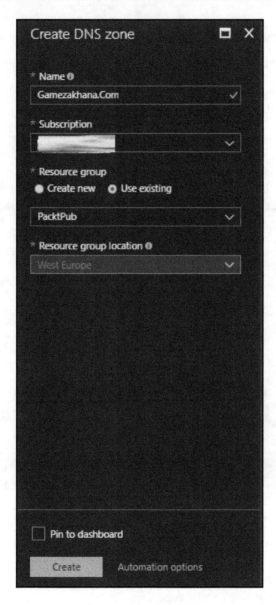

Figure 5.3: Create a new DNS zone

4. After clicking on **Create**, the DNS zone will be created within seconds.

Creating a DNS record

To create a DNS record, follow these steps:

1. Navigate to the DNS zone you have just created, as shown in the following screenshot:

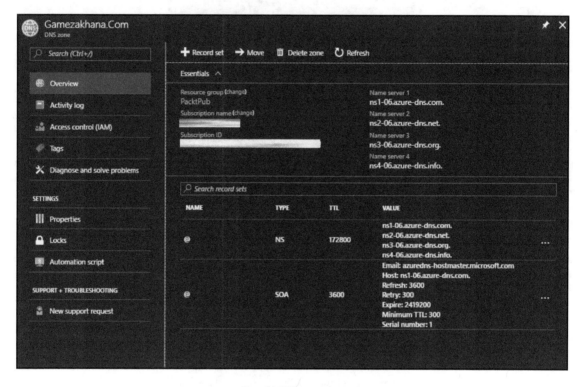

Figure 5.4: DNS zone overview

2. Click on **Record set**, and a new blade will be opened, asking to specify the following:
    - **Name**: The name of the record.
    - **Type**: The record type.
    - **TTL**: Time to live of the DNS request.
    - **TTL unit**: The measurement of time for TTL. It can be seconds, minutes, hours, days, or weeks.
    - **IP ADDRESS**: The IP address to which the record name will be translated.

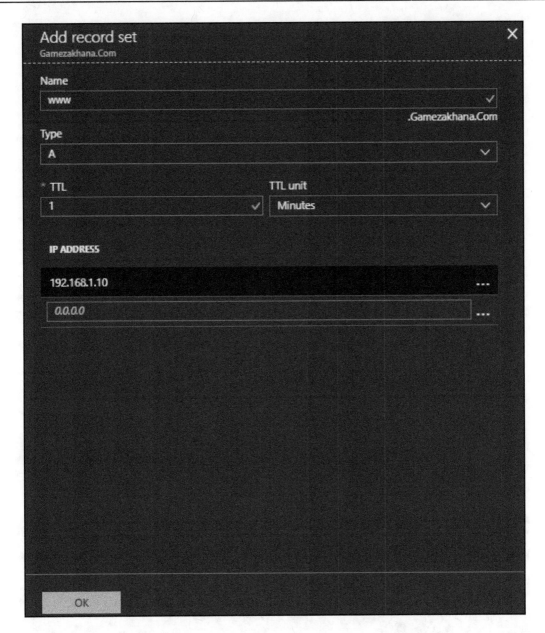

Figure 5.5: Create a DNS record

3. Once you click on **OK**, the record will be created within a moment.

4. You can view all the created records within this zone in the **Overview** tab, as shown in the following screenshot:

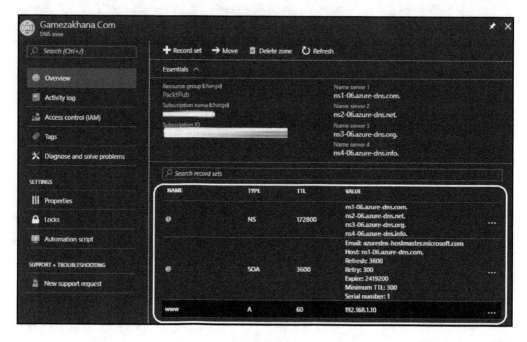

Figure 5.6: All the created records within the DNS zone

5. So far, the zone you have created cannot be translated externally. Therefore, you need to make sure that all Azure name servers are configured on your domain name, so the DNS records can be found on the internet, which will be discussed later:

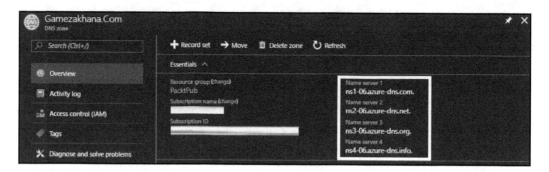

Figure 5.7: DNS zone name servers

DNS zones and records key points

The following key points are important for a better understanding of Azure DNS zones and records:

- Since the DNS zone location is global, you will not be asked during the DNS creation to specify the location of it.
- The DNS record propagation is very fast. Once it is created, it is propagated to Microsoft name servers.
- If you did not buy the domain name you have specified for the DNS zone, it will only be able to resolve the DNS queries directed to Azure DNS name servers.
- As of now, you cannot buy a domain name from Azure. However, you can get one from a third-party domain name registrar:
    - You can create 100 DNS zones per subscription
    - You can create 5000 record sets per zone
    - You can create 20 records per record set
- When you edit any DNS records, it might take about 60 seconds to get propagated to Azure DNS name servers. However, from the client side it would be cached if you have already resolved that record before, so you can either wait until the TTL is over or flush the DNS cache.
- Azure DNS can resolve IPv4 and IPv6 as well.
- You cannot create more than one DNS zone with the same name in one resource group, but you can do so by placing them in different resource groups.
- DNSSEC is not supported at the time of writing.

Azure DNS delegation

As mentioned earlier, your records will not be exposed externally by just building them in Azure, because you have to do some configurations from the domain registrar side to delegate Azure DNS. This will happen by changing the name servers used by the domain registrar by the name servers you used by the zone you have created in Azure.

If you have worked with DNS servers before, you should be aware that there are two types of DNS servers:

- **Authoritative**: This type can respond to the DNS queries from the records it has. For example, you might want to query `mail.yourcompany.com`, so you will be able to resolve this name to an IP address as long as it has a record created in your DNS zones.
- **Non-Authoritative (recursive)**: This type can use other authoritative DNS servers to do the DNS query for it. For example, if you want to open `www.packtpub.com`, the authoritative DNS server will not help because it knows nothing about other domains. However, the recursive one will call the authoritative to do that for it, and as a result you can browse the website.

In a nutshell, Azure DNS is authoritative DNS. As a result, it cannot be used to translate records by any machine in your on-premises, or even Azure VMs, because they are automatically configured to use recursive DNS.

Configuring DNS delegation for third-party domain names

You can configure DNS delegation by performing the following steps:

1. Create a DNS zone for the domain you want to delegate. In this scenario, I've got a domain name registered by GoDaddy. I've already created a DNS zone for it.
2. Then, navigate to the created DNS zone in the overview, and copy all the name servers to change the domain registrar name servers with these ones.
3. Navigate to the domain registrar domain manager to manage your domain name.
4. For GoDaddy users, they can access the domain manager via the following link: `https://dcc.godaddy.com/manage/dns?domainName=<your domain name>`.

5. Scroll down until you see the **Nameservers** section, as shown in the following screenshot:

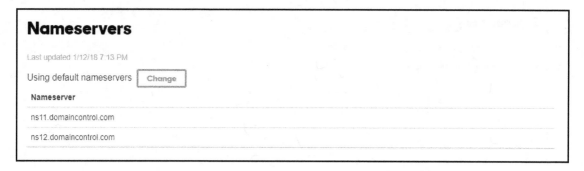

Figure 5.8: Domain registrar name servers

6. Click on **Change**.

7. Then, change the name server type to **Custom**, as shown in the following screenshot:

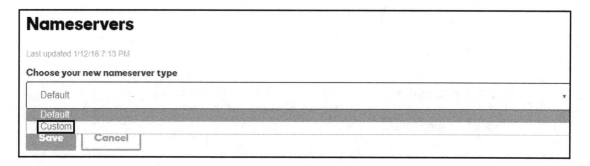

Figure 5.9: Domain registrar name server type

8. Then, add all the name servers for the Azure DNS zone and click on **Save**, as shown in the following screenshot:

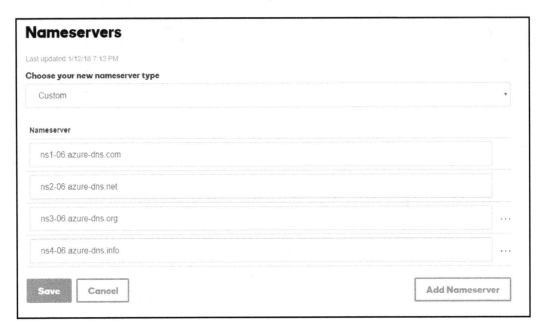

Figure 5.10: Enter Azure DNS zone name servers

9. Once saved, you will note that it will ask for confirmation by saving it again, until it gets changed to the custom name servers you have specified, as shown in the following screenshot:

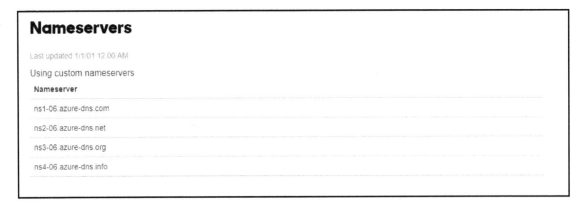

Figure 5.11: The current name servers

Configuring DNS delegation for subdomains

You might want to create a child zone for the zone you have created in Azure DNS and delegate that sub domain.

Doing so is not a different process, you only need to retrieve the name servers of the child zone and add them to the parent zone.

For a step-by-step guide, you need to perform the following steps:

1. Create a child DNS zone, as shown in the following screenshot:

Figure 5.12: Create a child DNS zone

2. Once the zone is created, navigate to it and copy the name servers of the child zone, as shown in the following screenshot:

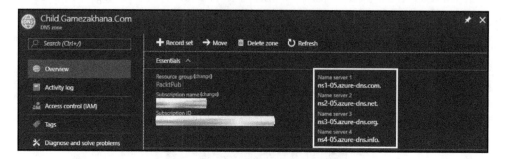

Figure 5.13: Child DNS zone name servers

3. Navigate to the parent zone and create a new record set adding the name servers' records of the child domain, as shown in the following screenshot:

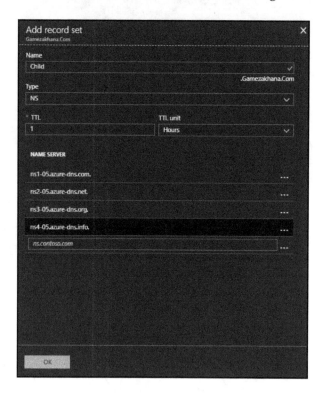

Figure 5.14: Adding the name servers' records of the child DNS zone

4. Once you have clicked on **OK**, it will take a moment to add the record set, and you should see the new record set of the child added, as shown in the following screenshot:

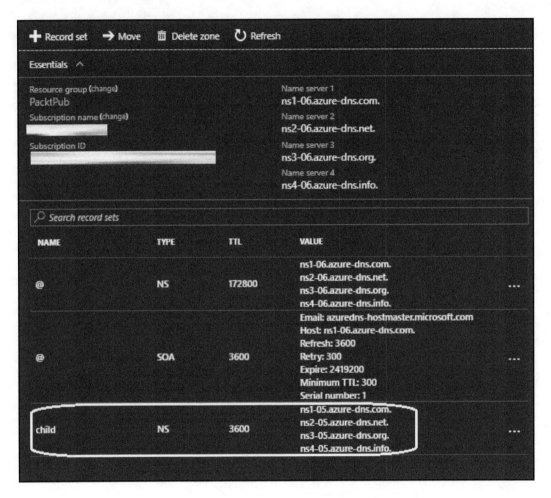

Figure 5.15: The record set has been added to the parent DNS zone

Azure DNS delegation key points

The following key points are important for a better understanding of Azure DNS delegation:

- When adding the name servers for delegation, it is recommended to add all the four name servers for higher availability and better resiliency. Also, in order to get Azure DNS SLA applied, you need to make sure that the four name servers are delegated.
- The domain registrar is the company that can provide an internet domain name, such as GoDaddy, Namecheap, Google, and so on.
- NS records are the responsible records for pointing to name servers.

Azure reverse DNS zone

Reverse DNS is still one of the most important DNS services, and it is no surprise that it is supported in Azure.

If you don't know too much about reverse DNS, in a nutshell, it does totally the opposite of what DNS does. So, instead of translating names to IPs, it translates IPs to names.

Configuring the reverse DNS zone has some slight differences to creating a forward DNS zone, which you will notice when performing the following steps:

1. Search for `DNS zones`, and click on **Add** to add a new one.
2. Fill the fields in **Create DNS zone**, as you have learned earlier, with only one change; for the **Name** field, you will write the DNS domain name IP address in a reverse way:
   - For IPv4, the name is written in the following format: `<IPv4 network prefix in reverse order>.in-addr.arpa`
   - For IPv6, the name is written in the following format: `<IPv6 network prefix in reverse order>.ip6.arpa`

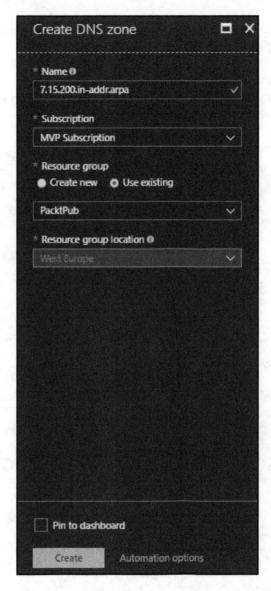

Figure 5.16: Creating a reverse DNS zone

3. Once the zone is created, you need to get it delegated from the parent zone, as you learned earlier.

4. Then, you can create the PTR records you want by clicking on the records set for the reverse zone and specifying the following:
    - **Name**: The rest of the IP address in reverse order
    - **Type**: **PTR**
    - **DOMAIN NAME**: The fully qualified domain name for the machine/service with that IP address

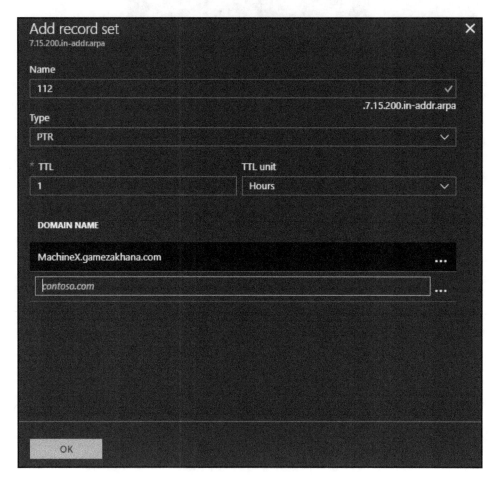

Figure 5.17: Creating a PTR record

Azure reverse DNS zone key points

The following key points are important for a better understanding of Azure reverse DNS zone:

- It's commonly known that to create a classless reverse DNS zone in a DNS server, you need to put a forward slash in the zone name. However, when you create the reverse zone in Azure, you will have to replace the forward slash with a hyphen, because Azure does not support zones with forward slashes in their names.
- Like IPv4 record set names for PTR records, IPv6 record set names must be written in reverse order.
- Zero compression is not supported for IPv6 while writing the record set name for a PTR record.

Private Azure DNS zones

Private zones is currently in preview, and in a nutshell, it does the common tasks that any DNS zone can do, but in a more customized way. So, you can assign the private DNS zone to a virtual network. As a result, you can do whatever you want to do within this virtual network with a DNS only associated with it, and you do not get the information within this virtual network exposed externally. Private DNS zones support most of the common DNS records.

To use private DNS zones, you need to send your subscription details to `AzureDNS-PrivateZone@microsoft.com`, since it is available in preview currently.

Also, creating private DNS zones and configuring DNS zones at the time of writing is only supported via PowerShell.

Therefore, in order to create a private DNS zone, you need to do the following:

1. Retrieve the VNet and store it in a PowerShell variable, as you've learned from the `Chapter 1`, *Azure Virtual Networks 101, Add Address Space to a Virtual Network using PowerShell* section.
2. Then, run the following cmdlet:

```
New-AzureRmDnsZone -Name InternalDNS.Private -ResourceGroupName
PacktPub -ZoneType Private -ResolutionVirtualNetworkId @($VNet.Id)
```

Where `$VNet` is the PowerShell variable that you have retrieved from the virtual network information for which you need to assign this DNS zone.

Private Azure DNS zones key points

The following key points are important for a better understanding of Azure Private DNS zones:

- Azure DNS supports split-horizon views for private DNS zones, so you can create an internal one for the virtual network, which will be queried by the virtual network only, and another one for the internet-facing queries.
- If you want to enable automatic registration for DNS records for any host within the virtual network, you have to replace the `ResolutionVirtualNetworkId` parameter with `RegistrationVirtualNetworkId`.

Automating the tasks

Let's automate the manual tasks that have been implemented so far.

Creating an Azure DNS zone using PowerShell

Creating an Azure DNS zone using PowerShell is pretty easy, you only need to run the following cmdlet:

```
New-AzureRmDnsZone -Name Gamezakhana.com -ResourceGroupName PacktPub
```

Creating an Azure DNS zone using Azure CLI 2.0

Like PowerShell, you can create an Azure DNS zone using Azure CLI 2.0 with only one command:

```
az network dns zone create --resource-group PacktPub --name Gamezakhana.com
```

Creating an Azure DNS record using PowerShell

To create an Azure DNS record using PowerShell, you need to create the `RecordConfig` and store it within a variable by running the following cmdlet:

```
$RecordConfig = New-AzureRmDnsRecordConfig -IPv4Address "192.168.1.55"
```

Then, you can create the record by running the following cmdlet:

```
New-AzureRmDnsRecordSet -Name www -RecordType A -ZoneName Gamezakhana.com -
ResourceGroupName PacktPub -Ttl 3600 -DnsRecords $RecordConfig
```

Remember that the TTL is expressed in seconds.

Creating an Azure DNS record using Azure CLI 2.0

You can create the DNS record by running the following command:

```
az network dns record-set a add-record --resource-group PacktPub --zone-
name Gamezakhana.com --record-set-name www --ipv4-address 192.168.1.56
```

Configuring Azure DNS delegation using PowerShell

If you want to configure the delegation with a third-party domain registrar, you will not be able to do the whole process using PowerShell, because PowerShell is not a supported API for this. However, you will need to retrieve the name servers of the Azure DNS zone, and you can do so by running the following cmdlets:

```
$GamezZone = Get-AzureRmDnsZone -Name Gamezakhana.com -ResourceGroupName
PacktPub

$GamezZoneRecords = Get-AzureRmDnsRecordSet -Name "@" -RecordType NS -Zone
$GamezZone
```

In case you want to delegate a subdomain, you have to create the child DNS zone first, as you have learned earlier, then you need to retrieve its DNS records and store it in a variable, as discussed in the previous cmdlets, and then finally run the following cmdlets:

```
$DelegateNSRecordSet = New-AzureRmDnsRecordSet -Zone $GamezZone -Name Child
-RecordType NS -Ttl 3600

$DelegateNSRecordSet.Records = $ChildZoneRecords.Records
Set-AzureRmDnsRecordSet -RecordSet $DelegateNSRecordSet
```

Where `$ChildZoneRecords` is the variable that you should create to store the child DNS zone NS records.

Configuring Azure DNS delegation using Azure CLI 2.0

To retrieve the NS records of the DNS zone to add them to the third-party domain registrar, you need to run the following command:

```
az network dns record-set list --resource-group PacktPub --zone-name
Gamezakhana.com --type NS --name @
```

To do the delegation for a subdomain, you need to create a child zone, as you've learned earlier.

Then, retrieve the child name servers by running the previous command for the child zone. After that, create a record set for name servers by running the following command:

```
az network dns record-set ns create --resource-group PacktPub --zone-name
Gamezakhana.com --name child
```

Finally, create an NS record by running the following command for each name server:

```
az network dns record-set ns add-record --resource-group PacktPub --zone-
name Gamezakhana.com --record-set-name child --nsdname ns1-03.azure-
dns.com.
```

Creating an Azure reverse DNS zone using PowerShell

Creating a reverse DNS zone is as the same as the forward DNS zone, except changing the format of writing the DNS zone name in this case, as discussed earlier. You can create it by running the following cmdlet:

```
New-AzureRmDnsZone -Name 77.12.200.in-addr.arpa -ResourceGroupName PacktPub
```

Then, you need to get it delegated from its parent zone.

Creating an Azure reverse DNS zone using Azure CLI 2.0

Creating the reverse DNS zone using Azure CLI 2.0 is pretty easy; you can do so by running the following command:

```
az network dns zone create --resource-group PacktPub --name 77.12.200.in-
addr.arpa
```

Then, you need to get it delegated from its parent zone.

Creating a PTR record using PowerShell

As discussed earlier, before creating any record using PowerShell, you need to create the configuration of it first and store it within a variable by running the following cmdlet:

```
$RecordConfig = New-AzureRmDnsRecordConfig -Ptrdname
"MachineY.Gamezakhana.com"
```

Then, you can create the record by running the following cmdlet:

```
New-AzureRmDnsRecordSet -Name 101 -RecordType PTR -ZoneName 77.12.200.in-
addr.arpa -ResourceGroupName PacktPub -Ttl 3600 -DnsRecords $RecordConfig
```

Creating a PTR record using Azure CLI 2.0

The PTR record can be created by running the following command:

```
az network dns record-set ptr add-record --resource-group PacktPub --zone-
name 77.12.200.in-addr.arpa --record-set-name 101 --ptrdname
MachineY.Gamezakhana.com
```

Summary

DNS is one of the most used services in all environments. Throughout the chapter, you should have learned how to work with Azure DNS services and its different capabilities, such as creating zones, and records, and delegating these zones, and even working with reverse DNS in Azure.

Next, we'll be covering one of the coolest Azure services, Azure Load Balancer, which is highly recommended to use to provide high availability for reaching out your applications.

Questions

- An Azure DNS zone can only operate within the resource group it is located in (true/false).
- If you do not add the four DNS zone name servers to the delegated zone, it will not work successfully (true/false).
- IPv4 and IPv6 are supported for reverse DNS (true/false).
- Private DNS zones can be assigned to the subnets (true/false).
- State and explain the two types of DNS server.
- Mention five of the benefits of Azure DNS.
- Write a PowerShell script that creates a DNS zone, and reverse DNS zone for the zone you have created with a PTR record. Remember that you have to get the reverse DNS zone delegated before creating the PTR record.

Further information

You can check out the following links for more information about the topics covered in this chapter:

- **Configure reverse DNS for services hosted in Azure**: https://docs.microsoft.com/en-us/azure/dns/dns-reverse-dns-for-azure-services
- **Import and export a DNS zone file using Azure CLI 1.0**: https://docs.microsoft.com/en-us/azure/dns/dns-import-export
- **How to protect DNS zones and records**: https://docs.microsoft.com/en-us/azure/dns/dns-protect-zones-recordsets
- **Use Azure DNS to provide custom domain settings for an Azure service**: https://docs.microsoft.com/en-us/azure/dns/dns-custom-domain

6
Azure Load Balancers

Introduction

In this chapter, you will be introduced to one of the most well-known high-availability solutions, which is Azure Load Balancer. Throughout the chapter, you will learn how to work with different types of Azure Load Balancer, and even how to configure them to fit your scenario, whether you have your load balancers accessed the via internet or on-premises.

Learning outcomes

The following topics will be covered:

- Introduction to Azure Load Balancer
- Azure Load Balancer flavors
- Hands-on with Azure Load Balancer

Introduction to Azure Load Balancer

Load balancing has always been one of the most important and straightforward methods for scaling up infrastructure.

The load balancer mainly distributes the traffic across a set of servers to enhance the responsiveness and the availability of VMs.

In a nutshell, the load balancer receives the traffic from the client and redistributes it across a set of servers. As a result, it ensures the following:

- High availability of the service for which you use Azure Load Balancer, as the client connects only to an online server that has no issues
- Flexibility of adding or removing backend servers behind Azure Load Balancer

Azure Load Balancer is not different. It is a layer 4 load balancer that distributes the traffic across either VMs or cloud services; and, if one of the VMs becomes unavailable, the traffic gets redirected to another VM.

Azure Load Balancer benefits

Azure Load Balancer has benefits that make it an attractive solution; the following points are some of the benefits:

- **Uses hash-based distribution mode**: This is the default mode for Azure Load Balancer, which is a 5-tuple hash that consists of the source IP, the source port, the destination IP, the destination port, and the protocol type which maps the traffic to the available servers. As a result, as long as the session is open, all of the packets within it will be directed to the same instance behind the load balancer.
- **Traffic control**: You can control the flow of the traffic by specifying that the inbound traffic that will come on a specific port will be directed to a specific port internally. For example, if you have an incoming request for the web server on port 80 on the public endpoint, but the web server behind the load balancer is configured to listen on port 3315, you can control that, as Azure Load Balancer supports port forwarding.
- **Awareness of the instances**: Azure Load Balancer is aware of not only the instance status, but also its number and whether it is scaled up or down, and it automatically reconfigures the load balancer whenever the number of instances changes.

Azure Load Balancer flavors

Azure Load Balancers can be classified based on performance (such as a basic load balancer or a standard load balancer) or purpose (such as a public load balancer for internet-facing scenarios or an internal load balancer for whatever you want to balance within your environment).

Basic Azure Load Balancer

This is the traditional Azure Load Balancer that has been around for a while. Throughout this chapter, plenty of information about this type is covered.

Mainly the basic load balancer does provide traffic distribution for the applications providing higher availability and better network performance. Considering that it detects the health state of the instances across which it distributes the traffic to make sure that the traffic is being distributed to the proper instances.

Standard Azure Load Balancer

The standard load balancer provides better resiliency and scalability. This type should unlock many scenarios, such as a 1,000-instance virtual machine scale set, availability zones, and so on. At the time of writing, this type is still in preview.

Standard Azure Load Balancer benefits

Standard Azure Load Balancer has many advantages; some of them are as follows:

- **Greater scalability**: This type of load balancer can server up to 1,000 VMs within a virtual network
- **Monitored service**: Using Azure Monitor, you can get vital insights that help in monitoring and even troubleshooting the environment
- **Higher security**: Now it is obligatory to associate an NSG with each VM with a standard load balancer

Public Azure Load Balancer

The public load balancer is also called an **internet-facing load balancer**. As its name implies, it is mainly used to load balance the requests coming from the internet. For example, all of the incoming traffic to the load balancer public IP address via a specific port will be mapped to the VMs in the backend, to their private IP and the port number.

Internal Azure Load Balancer

Unlike the internet-facing load balancer, this one is mainly designed for distributing the traffic across a specific subnet within a virtual network.

An internal load balancer can be used in the following scenarios:

- Intranet app running on Azure IaaS, for which you want to distribute traffic across the VMs on which the app is built.
- Cross-premises Azure virtual network, so that if you have a site-to-site VPN, you can have an internal load balancer set on a virtual network and distribute the incoming traffic from on-premises across the backend VMs.
- Non internet-facing machines. For example, you may have some virtual machines that do not have internet access, and you want to distribute the traffic across them.

Hands-on with Azure Load Balancers

Within this section, you will be working with Azure Load Balancers.

Creating a public Azure Load Balancer

Creating a public Azure Load Balancer is not a complicated process; you only need to follow the following steps:

1. Navigate to the Azure portal and search for `load balancer`, as shown in the following screenshot:

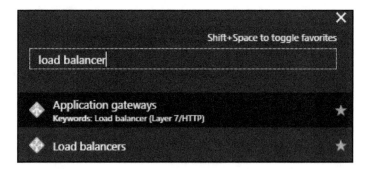

Figure 6.1: Searching for load balancers

2. A new blade will be opened, wherein all of the created load balancers should be displayed and from which you can create new ones. So, to create a new one, you need to click on **Add**, as shown in the following screenshot:

Figure 6.2: Load balancers blade

3. Once you have clicked on **Add**, a new blade will be opened, in which you have to specify the following:
   - **Name**: The name of the load balancer
   - **Type**: Whether it is **Internal** or **Public**
   - **Public IP address**: Specify the public IP address that will be used for the load balancer, by either selecting a pre-created one or creating a new one associated to the load balancer
   - **Add a public IPv6 address**: Tick this option if you want to use an IPv6 address in addition to the IPv4
   - **Subscription**: Select the subscription that will be charged for this service
   - **Resource group**: Specify the resource group on which the load balancer will exist

- **Location**: Specify the location on which the load balancer will be built:

Figure 6.3: Create a public load balancer

4. Click on **Create**, and within a minute, the load balancer will be created.

Creating an internal Azure Load Balancer

Creating an internal load balancer has some differences from the public one. Follow these steps, and you will know how to get it created:

1. From the **Load balancers** blade, click on **Add** again. In the new blade that opens, specify the following:
   - **Name**: The name of the load balancer.
   - **Type**: Whether it will be **Internal** or **Public**. Since in this case **Internal** will be used, you will note that some of the settings will be changed.
   - **Virtual network**: Specify the virtual network that contains the subnet across which the load balancer will distribute traffic.
   - **Subnet**: Specify the subnet that contains the VMs across which you want to distribute traffic.
   - **IP address assignment**: Specify the method of IP address assignment to the load balancer – whether the IP of the load balancer will be static or dynamic.
   - **Resource group**: The resource group on which the load balancer will exist.

- **Location**: Specify the location on which this service will be created:

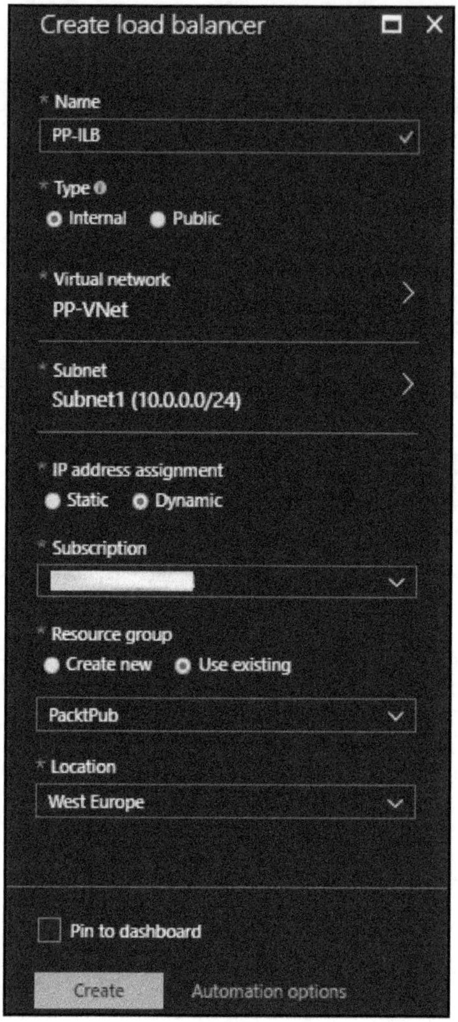

Figure 6.4: Create an internal load balancer

2. Click on **Create,** and the load balancer will be created within a minute.

Configuring public load balancer frontend IPs

When you create a public load balancer, you should specify a public IP address for it. However, you can add more public IPs to the load balancer to provide higher availability for the load balancer, and even use it to distribute the traffic across multipurpose VMs.

Creating a public IP address

Before getting started with this configuration, you need to make sure you have a un-used public IP address. So, let's get started by creating a new public IP:

1. Search for `public ip`, as shown in the following screenshot:

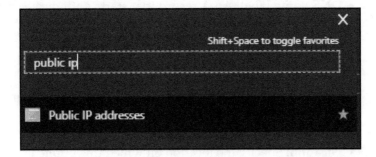

Figure 6.5: Searching for public IP address

2. The **Public IP addresses** blade will be opened. Click on **Add**, as shown in the following screenshot:

Figure 6.6: Public IP addresses blade

3. Once you have clicked on **Add**, the following blade will pop up, asking you to specify the following fields:

- **Name**: The name of the public IP. I recommend specifying a name that describes the purpose of the IP.
- **IP Version**: Specify the version of the IP address.
- **IP address assignment**: Specify whether you want it **Dynamic** or **Static**, taking into account that the static one costs more than the dynamic one. However, the static one is highly recommended for load balancers.
- **Idle timeout (minutes)**: The period within which the public IP will keep a TCP or HTTP connection open without relying on clients to send keep-alive messages.
- **DNS name label**: An **A** record that starts with the specified label and resolves to this public IP address will be registered with the Azure-provided DNS servers.
- **Create an IPv6 address**: Tick this option if you want this public IP to have an additional IPv6 address.
- **Subscription**: Specify the subscription that will be charged for using this IP.
- **Resource group**: Specify the resource group on which this IP will exist.
- **Location**: Specify the location on which this public IP address resource will be created:

Figure 6.7: Create a public IP address

4. Once you have clicked on **Create**, the public IP address will be created within a moment.

Add additional frontend IP

Now you can add the additional public IP to the public load balancer by following these steps:

1. Navigate to the public load balancer blade, as shown in the following screenshot:

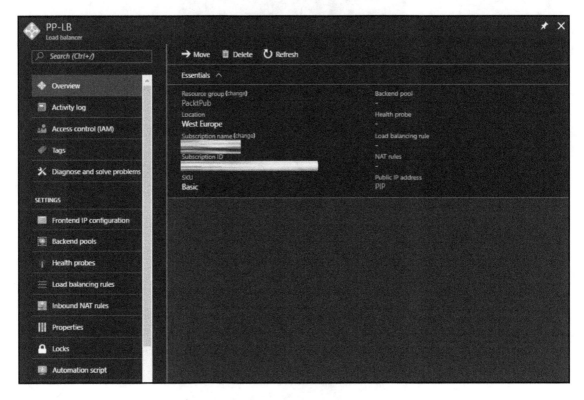

Figure 6.8: Public load balancer blade

2. Under **SETTINGS**, click on **Frontend IP configuration**, and the blade will display the current public IP associated with the load balancer, as shown in the following screenshot:

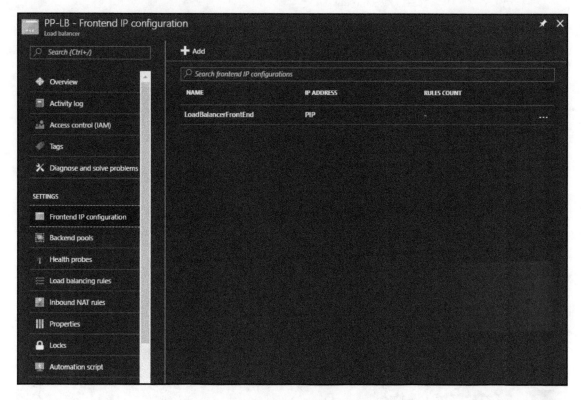

Figure 6.9: Frontend IP configuration

3. To add an additional public IP, click on **Add**, and a new blade will be opened, asking you to specify the following:
    - **Name**: Specify a name for the frontend IP
    - **IP version**: Specify its version – whether it is **IPv4** or **IPv6**

- **IP address**: Click on it, and a new blade will be opened where you can select the public IP you want to associate with the load balancer as a frontend IP:

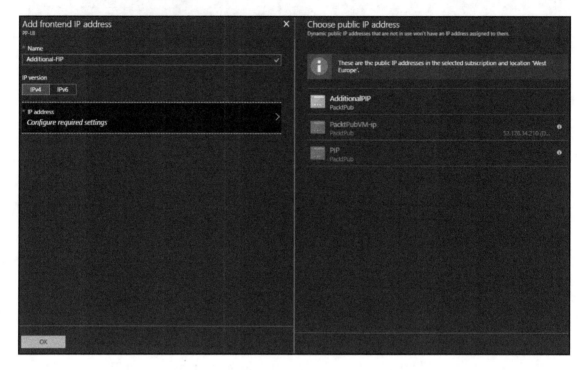

Figure 6.10: Add frontend IP address

4. Click on **OK**, and the IP will be added as a frontend IP within a moment.

Configuring internal load balancer frontend IPs

Unlike the public load balancer, the internal load balancer does not need a public IP address. Therefore, no public IPs will be created, and we will jump directly to the **Frontend IP configuration** of the internal load balancer and follow these steps:

1. Click on **Add**. A new blade will be opened, asking you to specify the following:
   - **Name**: A name for the additional frontend IP address.
   - **Subnet**: The subnet associated with the load balancer, from which you acquire an additional IP address for the load balancer.

- **Assignment**: Specify whether you need a dynamic IP or a static one for the load balancer. I recommend using a static one.
- **IP address**: If static is selected, you have to specify a static IP address within the range of the subnet:

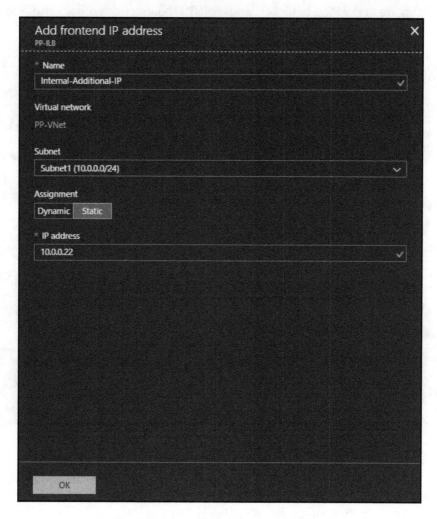

Figure 6.11: Add frontend IP address for the internal load balancer

2. Once you have clicked on **OK**, you will have the IP address added to the frontend IP addresses of the internal load balancer.

Configuring the load balancer backend pools

So far, you have configured the load balancer frontend part, but in this topic, you will learn how to configure the backend part, across which the traffic will be distributed:

1. Navigate to the load balancer; under **SETTINGS,** click on **Backend pools**, as shown in the following screenshot:

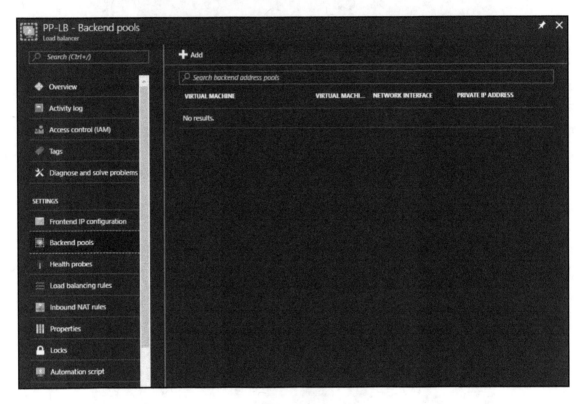

Figure 6.12: Backend pools

2. Click on **Add**, and a new blade will be opened, asking you to specify the following:
    - **Name**: The name of the backend pool.
    - **IP version**: Whether it is **IPv4** or **IPv6**.
    - **Associated to**: You can associate the load balancer with multiple VMs in an availability set, or a standalone VM, or a virtual machine scale set.

- **Target virtual machine**: Once you have decided which VM the load balancer will be associated with, you will note that more fields will be required to be filled. Since I've specified a single virtual machine in this scenario, I have to specify that machine.
- **Network IP configuration**: You should add the private IPs of the VM you have selected, and to do so, you need to click on **Add a target network IP configuration**:

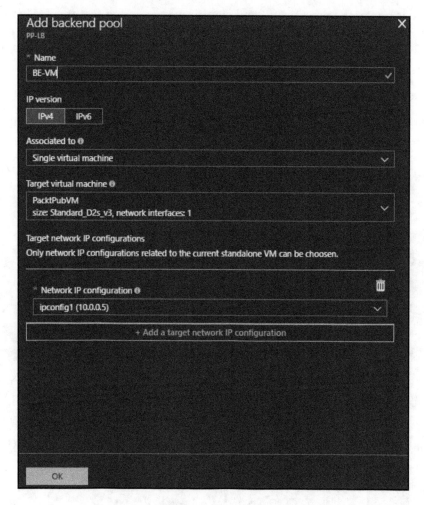

Figure 6.13: Add the backend pool

3. Once you have clicked on **OK**, it will take a couple of minutes to get it added.

Ensure that the VMs to which the load balancer is associated are not basic tier VMs and are in the same location as the load balancer.

For internal load balancers, only VMs within the same virtual network as the load balancers will be listed.

Configuring load balancer health probes

Health probe is one of the most useful and significant supported features for load balancers. With it, you can monitor the health of the VMs. So, if a VM goes down or is not reachable for any reason, the traffic will not be forwarded to the unhealthy VM, and get redistributed across other VMs.

To configure the health probes, you need to follow these steps:

1. Navigate to the load balancer; under **SETTINGS,** click on **Health probes**, and a new blade will be opened, as shown in the following screenshot:

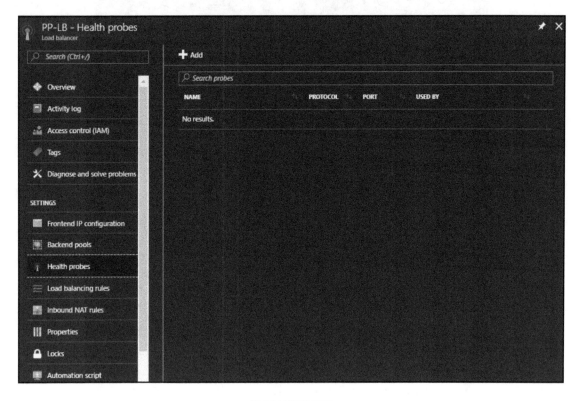

Figure 6.14: Health probes

2. Click on **Add** to add a new health probe to the load balancer, and a new blade will be opened, asking you to specify the following:
   - **Name**: Specify a descriptive name for the probe
   - **Protocol**: Specify whether it is HTTP or TCP
   - **Path**: If **HTTP** is selected as a protocol, you will have to specify the URI used for requesting the health status from the backend endpoint
   - **Port**: The port through which the probe will check the VM availability
   - **Interval**: The amount of time between probe attempts
   - **Unhealthy thresholds**: The number of consecutive probe failures that must occur before a virtual machine is considered unhealthy:

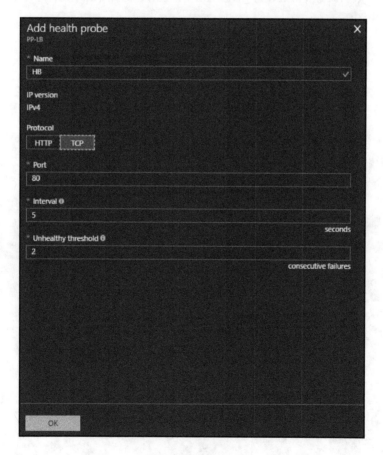

Figure 6.15: Add a health probe

3. Once you have clicked on **OK**, the health probe will be added

Configuring load balancing rules

Earlier in this chapter, we mentioned that you can control the incoming traffic by mapping a public port on the load balancer to a port on the backend address pool.

Such a way of control can be done with the load balancing rules.

 Before adding any load balancing rules, ensure that you already have one backend pool and one probe for the same load balancer you want to add a rule to.

To do so, you need to follow these steps:

1. Navigate to the load balancer; under **SETTINGS,** click on **Load balancing rules**, and a new blade will be opened, as shown in the following screenshot:

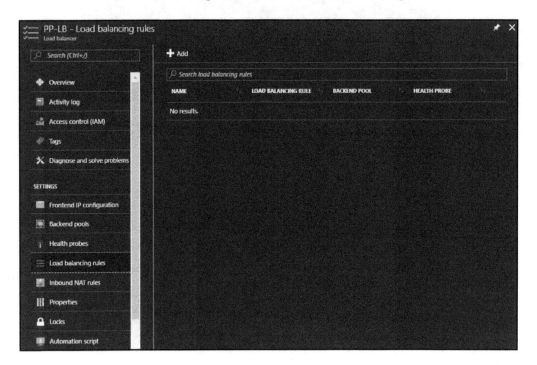

Figure 6.16: Load balancing rules

2. To add a rule, click on **Add,** and a new blade will be opened, asking you to specify the following:

- **Name**: Specify a descriptive name for the rule.
- **IP Version**: Specify the IP version for which this rule will be applied.
- **Frontend IP address**: Specify the frontend IP address through which the clients will communicate with this load balancer on the selected IP address, and the service will have their traffic routed to the target VM using this rule.
- **Protocol**: Specify the protocol that will be used by this rule.
- **Port**: Specify the port through which the client will come on the load balancer.
- **Backend port**: Specify the port opened for this service on the VM. It might be similar to the frontend port, or it might be different.
- **Backend pool**: The virtual machines in the selected backend pool will be the target for the load-balanced traffic of this rule.
- **Health probe**: The probe that will be used by this rule to determine which virtual machines in the backend pool are healthy and can receive load-balanced traffic.
- **Session persistence**: As long as the session between the client and one of the backend pool VMs is open, it will redirect all of the incoming requests from the client to the same backend VM. You can specify the following options for this setting:
  - **None**: This option will not enable the session's persistence
  - **Client IP**: This option will enable the session's persistence and will redirect any requests coming from the same client IP to the the same backend VM
  - **Client IP and protocol**: This option will enable session persistence and will redirect any requests coming from the same client IP and the same used protocol to the same backend VM
- **Idle timeout**: The period within which the TCP/HTTP connection will be opened without any active communication from the client.

- **Floating IP (direct server return)**: It is recommended to enable this feature only when configuring an SQL AlwaysOn Availability Group Listener. It can be enabled only when creating a rule, and if the port and backend port match:

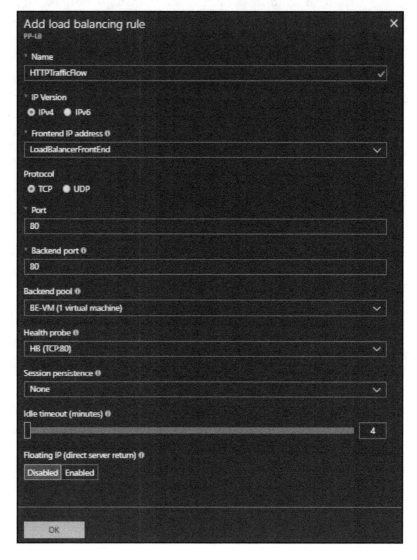

Figure 6.17: Add a load balancing rule

3. Once you have clicked on **OK**, the rule will be added within a couple of minutes.

Configuring inbound NAT rules

Another method for traffic control is the inbound NAT rules, which map a public port on the load balancer to a port on a specific virtual machine in the backend address pool.

To add an inbound NAT rule, you have to follow these steps:

1. Navigate to the load balancer; under **SETTINGS,** click on **Inbound NAT rules,** and a new blade will be opened, as shown in the following screenshot:

Figure 6.18: Inbound NAT rules

2. To add a new rule, click on **Add,** and a new blade will pop up, asking you to specify the following:

- **Name**: A descriptive name for the rule.
- **Frontend IP address**: The frontend IP address is the address through which the clients will communicate, then it will route their traffic to the target VM by this NAT rule.
- **Service**: You can scroll down and select one of the many services that are available in the drop-down list; if none of them are suitable for your service, you can select **Custom**.
- **Protocol**: If **Custom** is selected, you need to specify its type – whether it is **TCP** or **UDP**.
- **Port**: If custom is selected, you need to manually specify the port.
- **Associated to**: Specify whether it is associated with an availability set, a single VM, or a VM scale set.
- **Target virtual machine**: The VM that receives the traffic route by this NAT rule, taking into account that VMs must be in the same location as the load balancer.
- **Network IP configuration**: The IP configuration that will receive traffic for the chosen virtual machine, taking into account that the IP version of the IP configuration must match the IP version of the frontend IP address.
- **Port mapping**: If **Default** is selected, it will map the port through which the traffic comes to the same port on the VM. If custom is selected, you can manually specify the port to which the traffic will be routed:

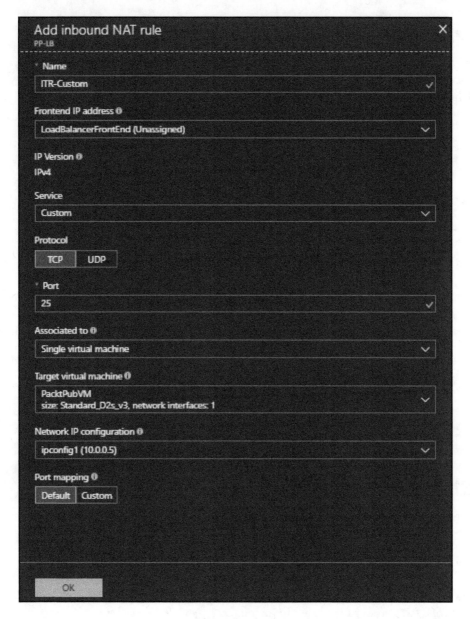

Figure 6.19: Add Inbound NAT rule

3. Once you have clicked on **Add**, the rule should be added within a couple of
   minutes.

Summary

By now, you should be aware of Azure Load Balancer types and how to work with them. This chapter has covered the most common tasks you need to know to work with Azure Load Balancers.

Coming up next: Azure Traffic Manager. It has some similarities with Azure Load Balancer regarding distributing the traffic.

Questions

- It is not obligatory to associate a basic load balancer with an NSG (true/false)
- Basic Azure VMs are supported to be associated with Azure Load Balancers (true/false)
- Enabling a floating IP for load balancing rules is only recommended for SQL AlwaysOn Availability Group listener (true/false)
- Azure Load Balancer uses hash-based distribution mode, that is, a 5-tuple hash. What are the five tuples?
- What are health probes?
- In a nutshell, explain the differences between basic load balancers and standard load balancers.
- State and explain two methods of traffic control for Azure Load Balancers.

Further information

If you are interested in knowing more about the topics that have been covered, you can check the following links:

- **Azure Load Balancer standard overview (preview)**: `https://docs.microsoft.com/en-us/azure/load-balancer/load-balancer-standard-overview`
- **Understand Load Balancer probes**: `https://docs.microsoft.com/en-us/azure/load-balancer/load-balancer-custom-probe-overview`
- **Configure the distribution mode for Azure Load Balancer**: `https://docs.microsoft.com/en-us/azure/load-balancer/load-balancer-distribution-mode`

- **Configure a load balancer for SQL Server Always On**: `https://docs.microsoft.com/en-us/azure/load-balancer/load-balancer-configure-sqlao`
- **Configure High Availability Ports for an internal load balancer**: `https://docs.microsoft.com/en-us/azure/load-balancer/load-balancer-configure-ha-ports`
- **Troubleshoot Azure Load Balancer**: `https://docs.microsoft.com/en-us/azure/load-balancer/load-balancer-troubleshoot`

7

Azure Traffic Manager

Introduction

In this chapter, you will be introduced to Azure Traffic Manager and its importance. You will learn about the components that will make it function properly, such as profiles, endpoints, and routing methods. Moreover, you will learn how to create and configure them. By the end of the chapter, you will have learned how to automate the manual tasks implemented throughout the chapter.

Learning outcomes

The following topics will be covered in this chapter:

- Introduction to Azure Traffic Manager
- Azure Traffic Manager routing methods
- Azure Traffic Manager endpoints
- Creating Traffic Manager profile
- Configuring Traffic Manager service endpoints
- Azure Traffic Manager key points
- Automating the tasks

Introduction to Azure Traffic Manager

So far, you have learned what Azure Load Balancer is and why it is important. Azure Traffic Manager is the next level of load distribution. With Azure Traffic Manager, you are not distributing your traffic across a VNet or a set of VMs, but you are distributing the traffic across multiple Azure data centers and multiple regions across the world.

Azure Traffic Manager is one of the Azure services that provide users better and more customizable solutions to control the user traffic distribution of various service endpoints located in different data centers around the world.

Azure Traffic Manager supports various endpoints, such as cloud services, App Services, and even public IP addresses that can be associated with VMs, Load Balancers, and so on. Also, it can be used with non-Azure endpoints, either in other clouds or in your on-premises environment. Azure Traffic Manager uses intelligent DNS to specify the fulfilling endpoint.

In a nutshell, Azure Traffic Manager is Microsoft's global application delivery solution that combines end-to-end application health checks, intelligent DNS, and global load balancing into a single platform.

Why Azure Traffic Manager?

Azure Traffic Manager has many benefits, and can help you achieve the following:

- **High availability**: The Traffic Manager ensures that the client request is getting directed to a healthy endpoint. Therefore, in the case that an endpoint goes down, it automatically failovers to a healthy one.
- **Better responsiveness**: The Traffic Manager can support the traffic distribution to a service endpoint that exists in different data centers across the world. As a result, Traffic Managers can direct the traffic to an endpoint that is nearest to the client, which will provide better responsiveness.
- **Maintenance with zero downtime**: Whenever you want to maintain some endpoints, you can do so, because traffic will be directed to the other endpoints; as a result, you will be up and running properly.
- **Distributing across Azure and external endpoints**: You can distribute the traffic not only to incorporate Azure services, but also to incorporate services that exist on your premises or in other clouds.

Azure Traffic Manager endpoints

To get the Traffic Manager service up and running in Azure, you need to create the Traffic Manager profile, which will be covered later. Within this profile, you will have to specify something called endpoints.

Endpoints are the receivers of the client requests that have been directed by Azure Traffic Manager.

Endpoints come in the following three flavors:

- **Azure endpoints**: These endpoints are used for Azure services, such as cloud services, App Services (for example, Web Apps), and public IP addresses that can be associated with a VM or a Load Balancer
- **External endpoints**: These endpoints are used for non-Azure services, that can be hosted either on your premises or in another cloud
- **Nested endpoints**: These endpoints can be used for larger and sophisticated environments wherein you have to create endpoints that refer to another Traffic Manager profile

Azure Traffic Manager routing methods

When the Traffic Manager receives the DNS query from the clients, it does not directly send it to the service endpoint, but it checks which routing method is being used, and based on that method it will determine to which service endpoint the request will be directed.

Azure Traffic Manager supports the following four routing methods:

- **Performance**: This method routes the client queries to the nearest endpoint based on the geographic location to the client, which will provide a better performance for the client because it follows the lowest network latency model
- **Weighted**: This method routes the client queries based on a weight that you define
- **Priority**: In this method, the queries will be queried to a primary service endpoint, and if it goes down, it will be redirected to a backup service endpoint
- **Geographic**: This method detects the region from which the DNS query is originated and redirects it to a specific endpoint

Creating Traffic Manager profile

To get the Traffic Manager up and running properly, you need to build a profile and specify its routing method and endpoints. Within this section, you will learn how to create a profile with the desired routing method. Without further ado, let's get started.

1. Navigate to Azure portal and search for `traffic manager`, as shown in the following screenshot:

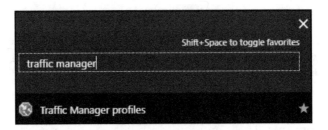

Figure 7.1: Searching for Traffic Manager profiles

2. Click on **Traffic Manager profiles**, and a new blade will be opened displaying the current profiles (if any), and from it you can add new Traffic Manager profiles by clicking on **Add**, as shown in the following screenshot:

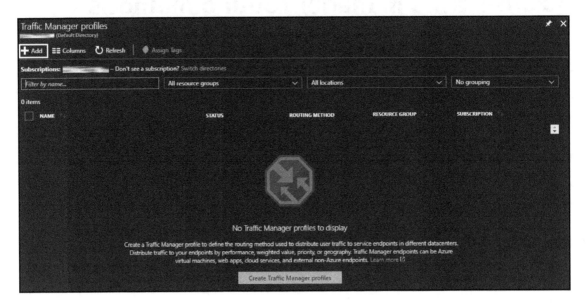

Figure 7.2: Traffic Manager Profile Blade

3. Once you click on **Add**, a new blade will be opened asking you to specify the following:

- **Name**: This will be the name for the Traffic Manager.
- **Routing method**: This is where you need to specify the routing method that would fulfill your needs according to what you have understood throughout the chapter.
- **Subscription**: This is where you need to specify the subscription that will be charged for using this service.
- **Resource group**: This is where you need to specify the resource group within which this service will exist as a resource.
- **Resource group location**: The location of the resource group in which the traffic manager will exist as a resource not as its location, because Azure Traffic Manager is a global service and not bounded to a specific region. However, like all Azure resources it needs a resource group to be stored in logically.

Figure 7.3: Create Traffic Manager profile

4. Once you click on **Create**, the profile will be created within a minute
5. Finally, you can create other Traffic Manager profiles with different routing methods, by following the same steps but changing the routing method to the one that fulfills your needs and suits your scenario

Traffic Manager configuration

Once the Traffic Manager profile is created, you can check its configuration by performing the following steps:

1. Navigate to the Traffic Manager you have just created, as shown in the following screenshot:

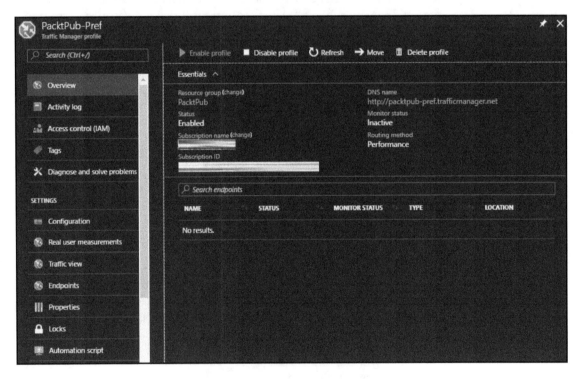

Figure 7.4: Traffic Manager overview

2. You can disable the profile by clicking on **Disable profile**, in the case that you do not need it at the time being but might need it later

3. Under **SETTINGS**, click on **Configuration** and the blade of configuration will be opened, wherein you can configure the following:

   - **Routing method**: You can change the routing method for this profile by clicking on the drop-down list and selecting the desired routing method.

   - **DNS time to live (TTL)**: When the client queries the Traffic Manager for the first time, it caches in the local cache, so the client does not have to go through the resolving process every time he tries to request something from the client. The value you specify here would be the period that the client can cache the Traffic Manager and has to update its DNS entries after this period again.

   - **Endpoint monitor settings**: These settings are responsible for monitoring whether the service is up and running or not. The settings are as follows:

      - **Protocol**: Here, you need to specify the protocol used by the endpoint, such as **HTTP**, **HTTPs**, and **TCP**.

      - **Port**: This is the port number via which the client accesses the endpoint service.

      - **Path**: The default is /, which means the root directory. However, you can enter a complete path with the filename.

   - **Probing interval**: This is the period after which the Traffic Manager will send a probe to make sure that the service is healthy. You have two options in the drop-down list, **30** seconds for normal probing and **10** seconds for fast probing.

   - **Tolerated number of failures**: Here, you need to specify the number of failures that can be tolerated before considering the endpoint as unhealthy.

- **Probe timeout**: This is the period after which the probe will be considered to have timed out.

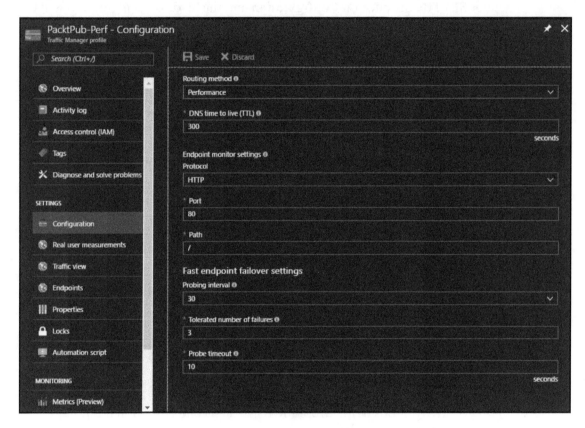

Figure 7.5: Configure the Traffic Manager profile

4. If you change any of these values, do not forget to click on **Save** to get these configurations applied

Configuring Traffic Manager service endpoints

So far, you have learned how to build the Traffic Manager with the desired routing method. However, you still miss the most important part, that is, endpoints. In this section, you will learn how to configure service endpoints for different routing methods.

Configuring endpoints for Traffic Manager with performance routing method

To configure the endpoints for Traffic Manager with the performance routing method, you need to consider that there are different types of endpoints.

Adding an Azure endpoint

Perform the following steps to add an Azure endpoint:

1. Navigate to the Traffic Manager profile, under **SETTINGS**, and click on **Endpoints**. A new blade will be opened, as shown in the following screenshot:

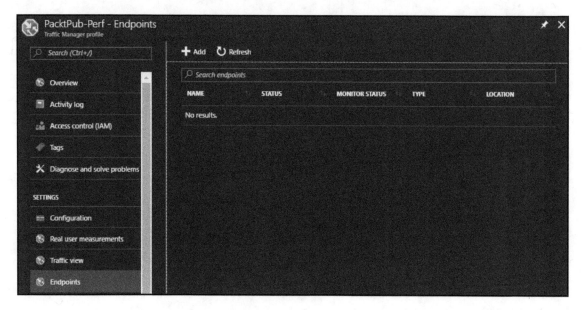

Figure 7.6: Traffic Manager endpoints

2. Click on **Add**, and a new blade will be opened wherein you need to specify the following:
   - **Type**: Here, the **Azure endpoint** would be selected. There are three types, which are as follows:
     - **Azure endpoint**: This will be used for Azure services, such as App Services and public IPs

- **External endpoint**: Here, you can specify external endpoints that are not even hosted in Azure
- **Nested endpoint**: This can be used to combine different Traffic Manager profiles together to create a customized scheme for traffic
- **Target resource type**: This option is available only for Azure endpoints wherein you need to specify the type for which the Traffic Manager will distribute the traffic. There are four types, which are as follows:
  - **Cloud Service**: It's a PaaS service and is still there for supporting the backward compatibility with classic Azure services that still use the ASM model
  - **App Service**: This includes Web Apps, mobile apps, and so on
  - **App Service slot:** This is similar to the slots used by web apps to make a staging environment
  - **Public IP address**: This type can refer to VMs or Load Balancers with public IP addresses
- **Target resource**: Whatever the type you select, you need to specify it by clicking on it, and a new blade will be opened from which you need to specify the resource
- **Add as disabled**: You can select this option to disable the endpoint for now, keeping in mind that you can enable it later

Public IP addresses must have the DNS name configured to be added as a target resource.

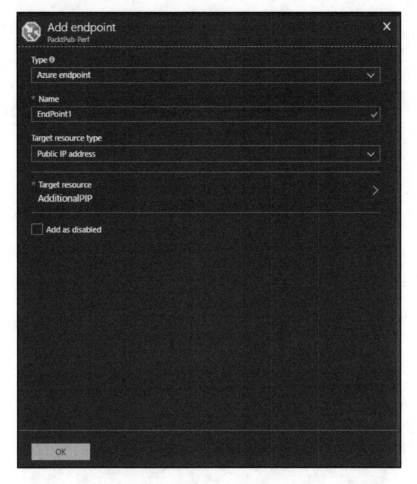

Figure 7.7: Adding an Azure endpoint

3. Once you click on **OK**, the endpoint will be added within a minute.

Adding an external endpoint

As mentioned earlier, the external endpoint can be on your premises or in another cloud. To add an external endpoint, you need to perform the following steps:

1. Navigate to the Traffic Manager profile, and under **SETTINGS** click on **Endpoints**
2. A new blade will be opened; click on **Add**

3. The blade for adding the endpoint will pop up, wherein you need to specify the following:

- **Type**: Here, the **External endpoint** would be selected
- **Name**: Here, specify a name for the endpoint
- **Fully-qualified domain name (FQDN)**: This is the FQDN of the endpoint, which might be a Load Balancer, a website, a VM, and so on
- **Location**: This is the location of the external endpoint

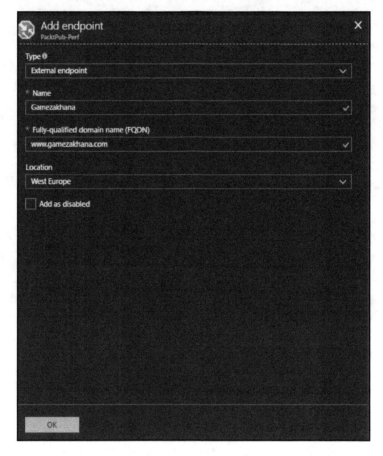

Figure 7.8: Adding an external endpoint

4. Once you click on **OK**, the endpoint should be added within a minute

Adding a nested endpoint

This type of endpoint combines more than one Traffic Manager profile with different routing methods for the environment that requires a complicated traffic routing. Perform the following steps and you will learn how to add nested endpoint:

1. Navigate to the Traffic Manager profile
2. Under **SETTINGS**, click on **Endpoints**; a new blade will open
3. Click on **Add** to add the endpoint, and a new blade will open asking you to specify the following:
   - **Type**: Here, select **Nested endpoint** from the drop-down list
   - **Name**: Here, specify a name for the endpoint
   - **Target resource**: Here, select the Traffic Manager profile you want it to be nested with
   - **Location**: Here, specify the location of the endpoint
   - **Minimal child endpoints**: This is the minimum number of the endpoints for the nested Traffic Manager profile to be able to receive traffic from the parent profile

Figure 7.9: Adding a nested profile

4. Click on **OK**, and the endpoint will be added within a minute

Configuring endpoints for Traffic Manager with the geographic routing method

As mentioned earlier, creating any Traffic Manager profile looks similar except for the routing method. So, in this section, we'll cover how to configure endpoints for traffic geographic profile. The following are the steps to be followed for configuration:

1. Navigate to the Traffic Manager profile and open it
2. Under **SETTINGS**, click on **Endpoints**, then click on **Add** in the endpoints blade
3. A new blade will pop up wherein you need to specify the following:
   - **Type**: Here, select the type that would suit your needs.
   - **Name**: Here, specify a name for the endpoint.
   - **Target resource type** (for Azure endpoints): Here, select the type you want according to your needs.
   - **Target resource** (for Azure endpoints): Here, select the resource for which you want to use this endpoint.
   - **Geo-mapping**: Here, specify the regions from which you want the traffic to be sent to this endpoint taking into consideration that you can specify a country within this region. In a nutshell, ensure adding the regions from which you expect traffic.

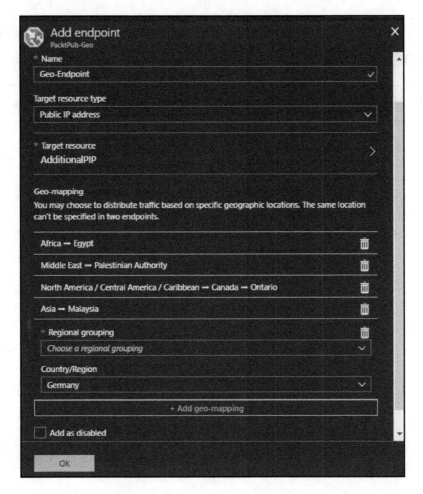

Figure 7.10: Adding an endpoint to a geographic Traffic Manager profile

4. Once you click on **OK**, the endpoint will be added within a minute

All the other types of endpoints can be added to the geographic Traffic Manager, the same as performance Traffic Manager endpoints, except with this type you will note that you need to specify the Geo-mapping for each endpoint type.

Configuring endpoints for Traffic Manager with the priority routing method

As mentioned earlier, this type of Traffic Manager follows the model of active-passive. In other words, when an endpoint with higher priority goes down, an endpoint with the lower priority will take its place.

Without further ado, let's get our hands with the endpoints for the priority Traffic Manager:

1. Navigate to the priority Traffic Manager profile
2. Under **SETTINGS**, click on **Endpoints**
3. A new blade will open; click on **Add** to add an endpoint
4. A new blade will open wherein you need to specify the following:
    - **Type**: Mention the endpoint type that would suit your scenario.
    - **Name**: Specify a name for the endpoint.
    - **Target resource type** (for Azure endpoint): Select the target type that would suit your scenario.
    - **Target resource** (for Azure endpoint): Select the resource for which you want to associate this endpoint with.
    - **Priority**: Specify the priority number of the endpoint. The lower the number, the higher the priority. Based on the priority, the primary endpoint and backup endpoints will be specified.

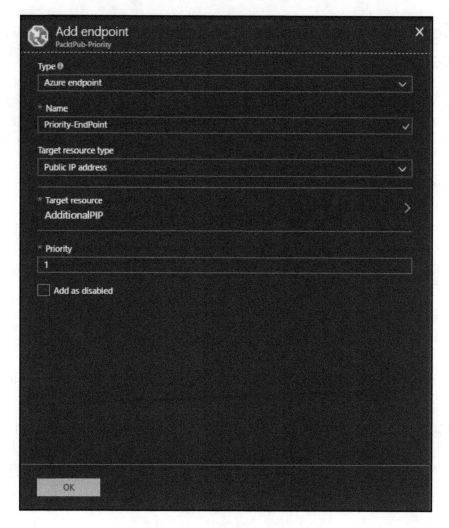

Figure 7.11: Adding an endpoint to a priority Traffic Manager

5. Once you click on **OK**, the endpoint will be added within a minute

All the other types of endpoints can be added to the priority Traffic Manager, the same as performance Traffic Manager endpoints, except with this type you will see that you need to specify a number for the priority for each endpoint type.

Configuring endpoints for Traffic Manager with the weighted routing method

As mentioned earlier, creating any Traffic Manager profile looks similar except for specifying the routing method. So, in this section, we'll cover how to configure endpoints for weight traffic profile. Unlike the priority Traffic Manager, this one specifies a number that implies that weight of endpoint, but all the endpoints can work in an active-active mode.

To configure the endpoints for the weighted Traffic Manager, you need to perform the following steps:

1. Navigate to the Traffic Manager profile.
2. Under **SETTINGS**, click on **Endpoints**. A new blade will be opened.
3. Click on **Add** on the endpoints blade. A new blade will be opened wherein you need to specify the following:
   - **Type**: Here, mention the type of endpoints that would suit your needs.
   - **Name**: Here, specify a descriptive name for the endpoint.
   - **Target resource type** (for Azure endpoint type): Here, select the target resource type that would suit your needs.
   - **Target resource** (for Azure endpoint type): Based on the target resource type you have specified, you can select the resource with that type.
   - **Weight**: Specify the weight of the endpoint. The lower the number, the higher the weight. If multiple endpoints have the same weight, the traffic will be distributed evenly among them. Otherwise, the endpoint with the lower number would have more odds to distribute the traffic.

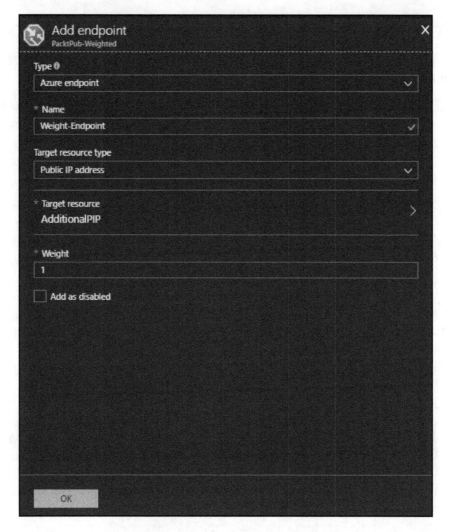

Figure 7.12: Adding an endpoint to a weighted Traffic Manager profile

All the other types of endpoints can be added to the weighted Traffic
Manager, the same as performance Traffic Manager endpoints, except
with this type you will see that you need to specify a number for the
weight for each endpoint type.

Azure Traffic Manager key points

The following key points should be the answers to the questions that came to your mind throughout the chapter:

- For priority Traffic Manager, you can specify a value for the priority between 1 and 1000.
- Multiple endpoints in priority Traffic Managers cannot share the same value.
- If you do not set the priority value, by default it will set the next in order.
- For weighted Traffic Manager, you can specify a value for the weight between 1 and 1000.
- If you do not set the weight value, by default it will be set to 1.
- For performance Traffic Manager, all the endpoints located within the same region will receive the traffic evenly.
- If any of performance Traffic Manager endpoints go down, the client traffic will be sent to the nearest endpoint.
- For geographic Traffic Manager, you can specify the regional grouping and the country/region. However, you can restrict the distribution only to some countries on the level of state/province, such as the USA, Canada, Australia, and the UK.
- You cannot assign a geographic Traffic Manager with the same geographic region to multiple endpoints.
- If the incoming traffic to a geographic Traffic Manager is coming from multiple endpoints, the lowest tier endpoint will be selected. For example, if you have an endpoint that receives traffic from Africa, and another one that has Egypt. Considering that the incoming traffic comes from Egypt, you will be directed to the Egypt endpoint.
- It's highly recommended to use nested endpoints for geographic Traffic manager with profiles that contain two endpoints at least.
- Disabled endpoints for geographic Traffic Manager will not be included in the region matching process.
- For any incoming traffic for geographic Traffic Manager from a nondefined region, Traffic Manager will return a **NODATA** response.
- Since Azure Traffic Manager works at the level of DNS, it cannot support sticky sessions, which means binding the user to a specific backend server.

Automating the tasks

Let's automate the manual tasks that have been implemented so far. All the automated tasks will be done for performance Traffic Manager; try to figure out how to use the other types.

Creating a Traffic Manager profile using Azure PowerShell

Creating the Traffic Manager profile using PowerShell is slightly different than the portal, because with PowerShell you need to specify some additional configurations. You can do so by running the following cmdlet:

```
New-AzureRmTrafficManagerProfile -Name PacktProfile -ResourceGroupName
PacktPub -TrafficRoutingMethod Performance -RelativeDnsName Packt -Ttl 30 -
MonitorProtocol HTTP -MonitorPort 80 -MonitorPath "/"
```

You can see that there is `Name` and `RelativeDnsName`. The difference between them is that the `Name` is the displayed name for the Traffic Manager, but `RelatvieDnsName` is the portion of the hostname that makes the following FQDN:
`http://packt.trafficmanager.net`

With respect to the other parameters, you saw them earlier in the Traffic Manager configurations section.

> When creating a Traffic Manager profile in the portal, the name you specify for the Traffic Manager profile is used as the name for `RelativeDnsName`.

Creating a Traffic Manager profile using Azure CLI 2.0

Creating a Traffic Manager profile using Azure CLI 2.0 does not require all the parameters required for PowerShell; it only needs the `RelativeDnsName`, but its format in Azure CLI is `unique-dns-name`. So, to get the Traffic Manager profile created using Azure CLI 2.0, you need to run the following command:

```
az network traffic-manager profile create --name CLIProfile --resource-
group PacktPub --routing-method Performance --unique-dns-name PacktCLI
```

Adding an Azure endpoint using Azure PowerShell

To add an endpoint to an existing Traffic Manager profile, you need to first retrieve the profile and store it within a variable by running the following cmdlet:

```
$profile = Get-AzureRmTrafficManagerProfile -Name PacktProfile -
ResourceGroupName PacktPub
```

Then, you need to retrieve the resource you want to distribute the traffic across. For example, a public IP address assigned to a Load Balancer. You can do so by running the following cmdlet:

```
$PIP = Get-AzureRmPublicIpAddress -Name "PIP" -ResourceGroupName PacktPub
```

Now, you can add the endpoint by running the following cmdlet:

```
Add-AzureRmTrafficManagerEndpointConfig -EndpointName LB1 -
TrafficManagerProfile $profile -Type AzureEndpoints -TargetResourceId
$pip.Id -EndpointStatus Enabled
```

Finally, do not forget to save that by running the following cmdlet:

```
Set-AzureRmTrafficManagerProfile -TrafficManagerProfile $profile
```

Adding an Azure endpoint using Azure CLI 2.0

You can add a Traffic Manager endpoint to Azure CLI 2.0 by running the following cmdlet:

```
az network traffic-manager endpoint create --name CLIEndpoint --profile-
name CLIProfile --resource-group PacktPub --type azureEndpoints --target-
resource-id <Enter the resource id>
```

Adding an external endpoint using Azure PowerShell

You can add an external endpoint by running the following cmdlet:

```
Add-AzureRmTrafficManagerEndpointConfig -EndpointName PSEndpoint -
TrafficManagerProfile $profile -Type ExternalEndpoints -Target
www.gamezakahana.com -EndpointLocation "West Europe" -EndpointStatus
Enabled
```

Adding an external endpoint using Azure CLI 2.0

Creating an external endpoint is similar to creating an Azure endpoint. All you need to do is, change the type, add the location, and specify the target. You can do this by running the following command:

```
az network traffic-manager endpoint create --name CLIEndpoint --profile-
name CLIProfile --resource-group PacktPub --type externalEndpoints --
target-resource-id <Enter the resource id> --endpoint-location westeurope
-target www.gamezakhana.com
```

Adding a nested endpoint using Azure PowerShell

To add a nested endpoint, you need to retrieve the child profile information and store it within a variable by running the following cmdlet:

```
$childEP = Get-AzureRmTrafficManagerEndpoint -Name childEP -
ResourceGroupName PacktPub -Type AzureEndpoints -ProfileName PacktProfile
```

Then, you can create it by running the following cmdlet:

```
New-AzureRmTrafficManagerEndpoint -Name child-endpoint -ProfileName
PacktProfile -ResourceGroupName PacktPub -Type NestedEndpoints -
TargetResourceId $childEP.Id -EndpointStatus Enabled -EndpointLocation
"West Europe" -MinChildEndpoints 1
```

Adding a nested endpoint using Azure CLI 2.0

You can add a nested endpoint by running the following command – consider changing the parameters' values to your values:

```
az network traffic-manager endpoint create --name CLIEndpoint --profile-
name CLIProfile --resource-group PacktPub --type externalEndpoints --
target-resource-id <Enter the resource id> --endpoint-location westeurope --
target childprofile.trafficmanager.net --min-child-endpoints 1
```

Summary

This chapter has covered one of the most important enterprise networking solutions. By now, you should know how to use Azure Traffic Manager and design a solution that would suit your environment.

The next chapter will cover, Azure Application Gateway, which has some similarities with Azure Load Balancer and Azure Traffic Manager regarding traffic distribution.

Questions

- Azure Traffic Manager works on the DNS level (true/false)
- Azure Traffic Manager supports only Azure services (true/false)
- Sticky sessions are not supported for Azure Traffic Manager (true/false)
- The higher the number you assign to a priority Traffic Manager, the higher will be the priority (true/false)
- State and explain the Traffic Manager routing methods
- State the endpoints' types
- Write a PowerShell script that creates a performance Traffic Manager profile, with three endpoints associated to it (Azure endpoint, external endpoint, and nested endpoint)

Further information

If you are interested to learn more about the topics that have been covered, you can check the following links:

- **Country/region hierarchy used by Azure Traffic Manager for geographic traffic routing method:** https://docs.microsoft.com/en-us/azure/traffic-manager/traffic-manager-geographic-regions
- **How Traffic Manager works:** https://docs.microsoft.com/en-us/azure/traffic-manager/traffic-manager-overview#how-traffic-manager-works
- **Nested Traffic Manager profile examples:** https://docs.microsoft.com/en-us/azure/traffic-manager/traffic-manager-nested-profiles

- **How to send real user measurements to Azure Traffic Manager using web pages**: https://docs.microsoft.com/en-us/azure/traffic-manager/traffic-manager-create-rum-web-pages
- **Performance considerations for Traffic Manager**: https://docs.microsoft.com/en-us/azure/traffic-manager/traffic-manager-performance-considerations
- **Point a company internet domain to an Azure Traffic Manager domain**: https://docs.microsoft.com/en-us/azure/traffic-manager/traffic-manager-point-internet-domain
- **Troubleshooting a degraded state on Azure Traffic Manager**: https://docs.microsoft.com/en-us/azure/traffic-manager/traffic-manager-troubleshooting-degraded

8

Azure Application Gateway

Introduction

Our journey with this book is coming to an end. In this chapter, we'll cover the last topic of the book, that is, the Azure Application Gateway. Throughout this chapter, you will get to know what it is and why you should use it. Also, you will learn about its types and the different scenarios when you can use it. Moreover, you will find a step-by-step guide about how to work with it.

Learning outcomes

The following topics will be covered:

- An introduction to Azure Application Gateway
- Creating an Azure Application Gateway
- Configuring Azure Application Gateway settings

An introduction to Azure Application Gateway

In 2015, Microsoft announced one of its coolest and important enterprise networking solutions in Azure, named Azure Application Gateway, and ever since then, this service has witnessed many enhancements based on customers' feedback.

Azure Application Gateway is a layer 7 load balancing service for applications. This service comes with many features for customers using web applications, such as SSL and CPU offloading. Also, it provides a **web application firewall** (**WAF**) included in it that provides protection for the web applications and prevention of malicious attacks.

Why Azure Application Gateway?

Azure Application Gateway has many features that would help you to use it in more advanced scenarios. The following are some of the most common features of Azure Application Gateway:

- **HTTP/HTTPS load balancing**: Azure Application Gateway provides a layer 7 round-robin load balancing for HTTP/HTTPS incoming traffic.
- **SSL overhead offloading**: The web servers do not have to decrypt the HTTPS connection when using Azure Application Gateway, as it decrypts the traffic when it is received and sends the traffic unencrypted. As a result, the web servers get a better performance.
- **WAF**: Azure Application Gateway can be used as a web application firewall in order to protect Azure Web Apps, such as session hijacks and SQL injection.
- **End-to-end SSL encryption**: Decrypting the traffic at the application gateway does not mean that the traffic can be sent to the web servers unencrypted. You can re-encrypt the traffic from the application gateway to the backend server and from the backend server to the client using routing rules.
- **Cookie-based session affinity**: You can stick a user session to the same backend server using this feature, as application gateway can use the gateway-managed cookies to direct all the traffic coming from the same user session to the same backend server. This feature is highly beneficial in cases, such as web mail servers and shopping carts apps.

- **WebSocket support**: You might have web applications that support real-time functioning in both directions between the client and the web server.
- **Multi-site routing**: You can use single application gateway capabilities for multiple websites up to 20 websites.
- **Health monitoring**: You can monitor the backend servers using health probes to check the status of the servers/applications.
- **URL-based content routing**: Azure Application Gateway can logically distribute the traffic between the backend servers according to incoming traffic based on the URL path.

In a nutshell, Azure Application Gateway is built on a dedicated virtual appliance that is fully managed by Microsoft providing an application delivery controller as a service.

The flavors of Azure Application Gateway

Azure Application Gateway comes in the following two flavors:

- **Standard**: This flavor does the most common tasks of Azure Application Gateway, and most of the previously mentioned features are available when using this flavor. However, the other features that provide protection from and prevention of attacks are not available in this flavor.
- **WAF**: This flavor provides all the features supported by the standard flavor in addition to the protection from attacks and web vulnerabilities prevention.

These two flavors are available in three sizes: small, medium, and large. Remember that small is only recommended to be used for Dev/Test scenarios.

For more information about the pricing of the different flavors, you can check https://azure.microsoft.com/en-us/pricing/details/application-gateway/.

Creating an Azure Application Gateway

Creating an Azure Application Gateway is a simple process, and you can learn how to do it by following these steps:

1. Navigate to the Azure portal and search for `application gateway`, as shown in the following screenshot:

Figure 8.1: Searching for application gateways service

2. Once you have clicked on **Application gateways**, a new blade will be opened wherein all the application gateways that have been created (if any) should be displayed and from where you can add new application gateways by clicking on **Add**, as shown in the following screenshot:

Figure 8.2: Application gateways blade

3. Once you have clicked on **Add**, a new blade will be opened wherein you have to specify the following:
    -   **Name**: Specify a descriptive name for the application gateway.
    -   **Tier:** Specify which flavor you are going to use.
    -   **SKU size**: Select the SKU size that would fit your scenario.
    -   **Instance count**: To be covered by application gateway SLA, you need to make sure there are at least two instances specified. The higher the number of instances, the better the performance of the application gateway. Remember that you cannot specify instances more than 10.
    -   **Subscription**: Specify the subscription that will be charged for using this service.
    -   **Resource group**: Specify the resource group in which this service will exist as a resource.
    -   **Location**: Specify the location where this service will be created.

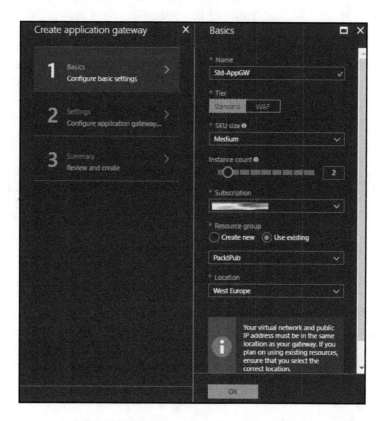

Figure 8.3: Configure the basic settings for Azure Application Gateway

4. Once you have clicked on **OK**, you will be navigated to the next blade wherein you have to specify the following:

- **Virtual network**: Specify a virtual network to be used with the application gateway. Ensure that it contains an empty subnet or a subnet with no other resource types besides application gateways.
- **Subnet**: When you select the virtual network, all the empty subnets within this VNet will be available in the drop-down list, so you can select one of them.
- **Frontend IP configuration**: Azure Application Gateway can either work facing the internet or in the internal networks. Based on your case, you need to specify the following:
    - **IP address type**: You can select **Public** for internet facing scenarios or **Private** for internal networks.
    - **Public IP address**: If **Public** is selected as a type, you need to specify the public IP address that will act as a frontend IP address for the application gateway. If **Private** is selected, you can specify the static private IP address that will be used for the application gateway by ticking this option. Otherwise, a dynamic private IP address will be assigned to the application gateway.
- **Listener configuration**: You need to specify the following for the listener configuration:
    - **Protocol**: You can either use HTTP or HTTPS. At the moment, only these two protocols are supported to be used with the application gateway. If HTTPS is selected, you will have to upload its PFX certificate and specify the user name and password for this certificate.
    - **Port**: Specify the port number on which the application gateway will listen to the traffic.
- **Upgrade to WAF tier**: You can upgrade this tier from standard to WAF by ticking this option, then you will have to specify the following:
    - **Firewall status**: You can either select **Enable** to get it up and running once the application gateway is created, or you can select **Disable** to get it disabled for now and enabling it later when you need it.

- **Firewall mode**: If **Enabled** is selected, you will have to specify the mode of the firewall. Either it will work for detection or prevention.

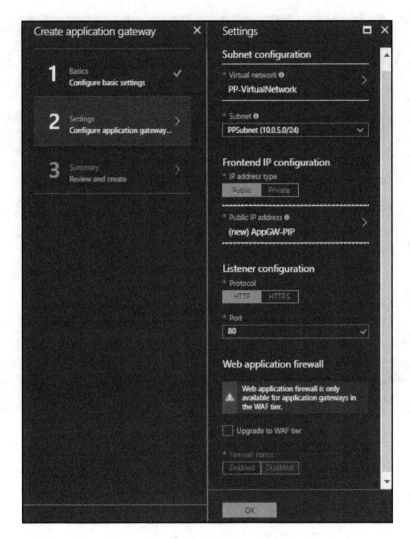

Figure 8.4: Configure application gateway settings

5. Once you have clicked on **OK**, a **Summary** blade will be opened displaying all the settings you have specified. So, you can check its configuration before you upgrade to avoid any misconfiguration:

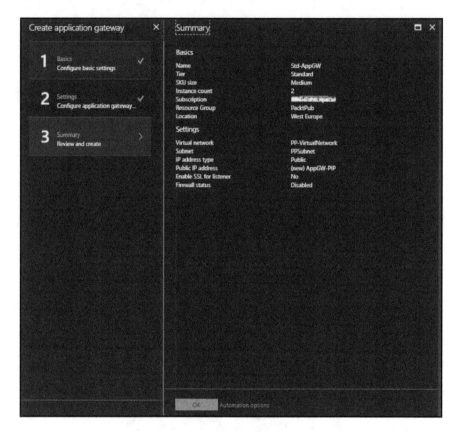

Figure 8.5: Application gateway settings summary

6. Once you have clicked on **OK**, the creation process of the application gateway will start. Remember that it will take a while to get up and running.

Creating a WAF application gateway will require no additional settings other than specified within this section. However, you will have to change the tier from **Standard** to WAF, if, you selected **Standard** and want it to work as WAF also, you can do it while configuring the settings. Later in this chapter, you will learn how to upgrade a created standard application gateway to WAF.

Configuring Azure Application Gateway settings

Azure Application Gateway has many settings that need to be configured to fully utilize its attractive features.

Azure Application Gateway configurations

You can manipulate some of the application gateway configurations, such as the tier, SKU size, and instance count by following the steps:

1. Navigate to the created application gateway, as shown in the following screenshot:

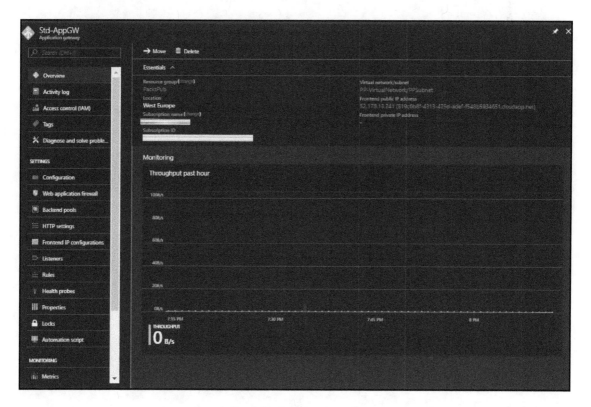

Figure 8.6: Application gateway overview

2. Under **SETTINGS**, click on **Configuration**, and a new blade will be opened, as shown in the following screenshot:

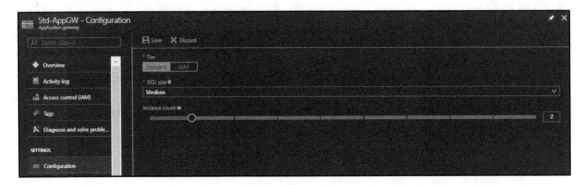

Figure 8.7: Azure Application Gateway configurations

3. On the previous blade, you can change the following:
   - **Tier**: You can upgrade it to WAF if it is **Standard** or downgrade to **Standard** if it is **WAF**.
   - **SKU size**: You can change the size to the size that would fit your environment anytime you want. So, if you selected **Medium** and your environment keeps growing, you can change it to **Large**.
   - **Instance count**: You can increase and decrease the number of instances whenever you want according to your needs.

4. Once you have changed the configurations to fit your needs, do not forget to click on **Save** to let the application gateway work with the new changes.

Configuring WAF

You can configure the settings of the WAF by following these steps:

1. Navigate to the application gateway.
2. Under **SETTINGS**, click on **Web application firewall**, and a new blade will be opened. In this scenario, it is a standard application gateway that will be upgraded to WAF:

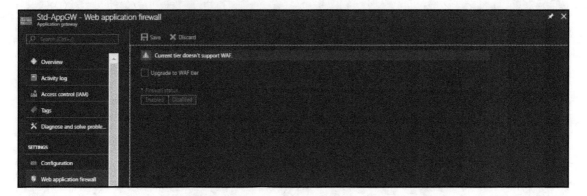

Figure 8.8: The web application firewall configuration blade

3. To upgrade the application gateway to WAF, you need to tick **Upgrade to WAF tier**. Then, you will have to specify the following settings:
    - **Firewall status**: You can specify whether you want to enable it or disable it by selecting the status you want. If it is enabled, you will be able to configure its settings.
    - **Firewall mode**: Specify whether you want the firewall to work in **Detection** or **Prevention** mode.
    - **Rule set**: The protections provided for Azure Application Gateway (WAF) are provided by the **Open Web Application Security Project (OWASP)**. At the moment, it supports two versions of OWASP. So, if you click on the drop-down list, you can select **OWASP 3.0** or **OWASP 2.2.9**.

- **Advanced rule configuration**: By default, all the rules of the rule set you select will be applied. However, if you want to customize these rules, you can select this option. As a result, all the rules of the rule set will be displayed, and you can unselect the rule if you do not want to get it applied.

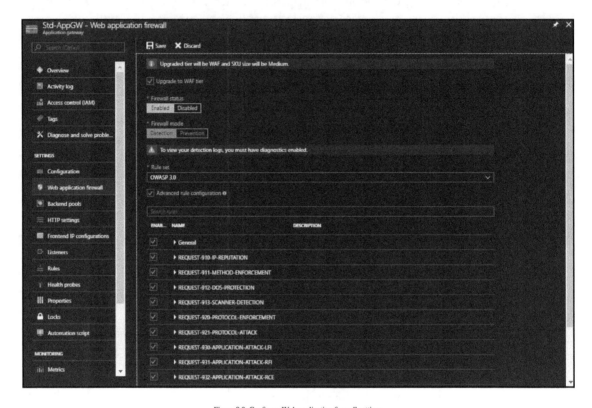

Figure 8.9: Configure Web application firewall settings

4. Once you are done with the configurations, do not forget to click on **Save**, and the application gateway will be upgraded to WAF.

Configuring the backend pool

By now, you should configure the backend pool for the application gateway. To do so, you need to follow the steps:

1. Navigate to the application gateway.
2. Under **SETTINGS**, click on **Backend pools**, and a new blade will be opened, as shown in the following screenshot:

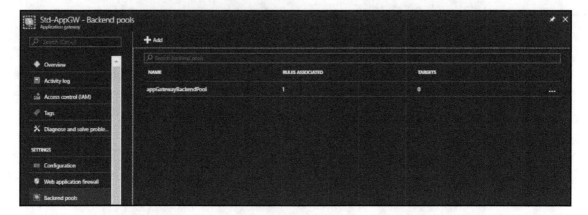

Figure 8.10: Backend pools

3. You will see that there is a backend pool created named `appGatewayBackendPool` but with no targets. So, in order to add a target for it, you have to click on it and a new blade will be opened, as shown in the following screenshot:

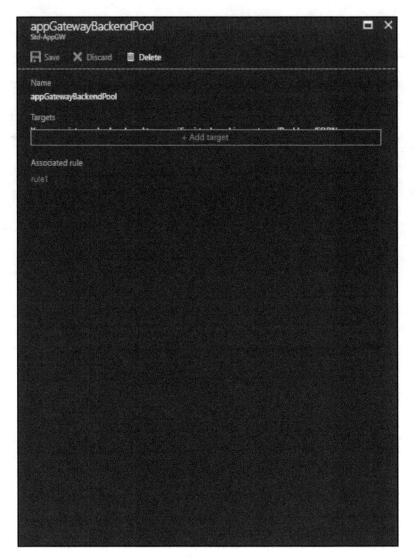

Figure 8.11: The backend pool profile

4. To add targets to the backend pool, you have to click on **Add target**. Then, you need to specify the type of the target. Either by entering the **IP address or FQDN**, as shown in the following screenshot:

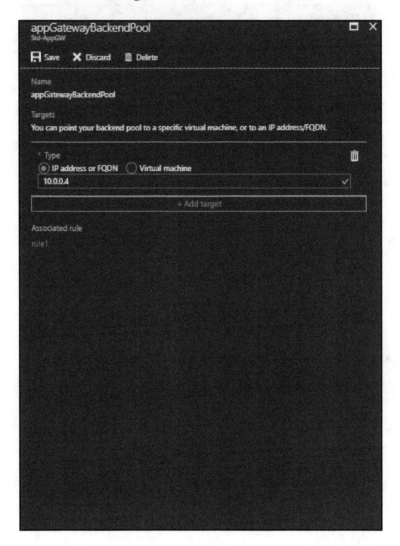

Figure 8.12: Add a target with its IP address

5. Or you can select the **Virtual Machine** option, and the network IP network configuration associated with it, as shown in the following screenshot:

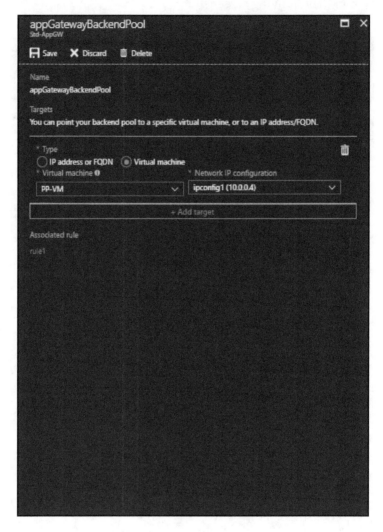

Figure 8.13: Add a VM target

6. You can add more targets by clicking on **Add target** and specifying them, as you have learned in this section.

7. Also, you can add another backend pool by clicking on **Add** on the **Backend pool** blade and specify the target for this backend pool.

Configuring Azure Application Gateway HTTP settings

To do some manipulations to the HTTP settings of the application gateway, you need to perform the following steps:

1. Navigate to the application gateway.
2. Under **SETTINGS**, click on **HTTP settings**, as shown in the following screenshot:

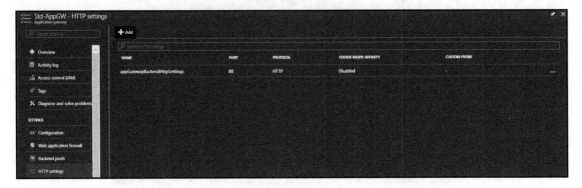

Figure 8.14: Application gateway HTTP settings

3. You will note that by default there settings already added, which can be changed by clicking on it and changing the settings, or you can click on **Add** to add a new HTTP settings.
4. When you click on **Add**, a new blade will be opened wherein you have to specify the following:
    - **Name**: Specify a descriptive name for the settings.
    - **Cookie-based affinity**: Specify whether you want to enable this feature or not.
    - **Request timeout**: Specify the period after which the request will be considered as timed-out.
    - **Protocol**: Select the protocol that would fit your application, whether it is **HTTP** or **HTTPS**. If **HTTPS** is selected, you would need to specify a name for the certificate and upload the CER certificate that would be used to authenticate the backend servers.

- **Use custom probe**: If you have custom probes created, you can select this option. Later in this chapter, you will learn how to create custom probes.

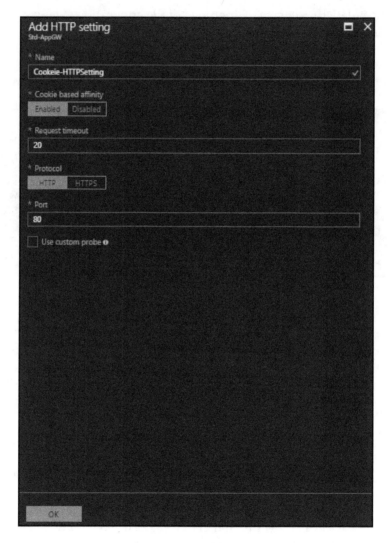

Figure 8.15: Configure HTTP settings

5. Once you have clicked on **OK**, the HTTP settings will be added.

Configuring frontend IP configurations

As mentioned earlier, Azure Application Gateway can be facing the internet or working for internal networks. So, to understand the frontend IP configurations, you need to follow these steps:

1. Navigate to the application gateway.
2. Under **SETTINGS**, click on **Frontend IP configurations**, and a new blade will be opened, as shown in the following screenshot:

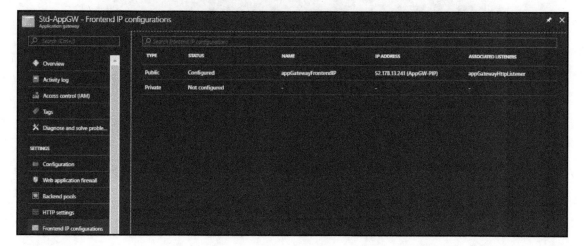

Figure 8.16: Frontend IP configurations

3. To configure the private frontend IP, you have to click on it, and a new blade will be opened where you have to specify the following:
   - **Name**: Specify a descriptive name for it.
   - **Choose a specific private IP address**: You can select this option to specify a static private IP address. Otherwise, the private IP address will be dynamically assigned.

Figure 8.17: Configure private frontend IP address

4. Once you are done, you need to click on **Save** to apply the changes.

Configuring listeners

Listeners are used to route the traffic from the application gateway to the backend pool. There are two types of listeners:

- **Basic**: This can be associated with only one rule that means it can be assigned to only one site
- **Multi-site**: As the name implies, this listener can be associated with multiple rules, which means that it can be assigned to multiple sites

Configuring basic listener

To configure the basic listener, you need to follow these steps:

1. Navigate to the application gateway.
2. Under **SETTINGS**, click on **Listeners**, and a new blade will be opened, as shown in the following screenshot:

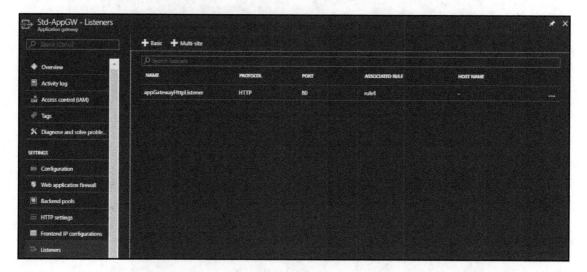

Figure 8.18: Listeners

3. To add a basic listener, click on **Basic**, and a new blade will be opened wherein you have to specify the following:
    - **Name**: Specify a descriptive name for the listener
    - **Frontend IP configuration**: Select the frontend IP configuration you want to associate with this listener
    - **Frontend port**: Since no frontend ports have been created in this scenario, a new one will be created by specifying the following:
        - **Name**: Specify a descriptive name for the frontend port
        - **Port**: Specify the port number on which it will listen to the traffic

- **Protocol**: Specify the protocol that would be used for your case. Either it will be **HTTP** or **HTTPS**

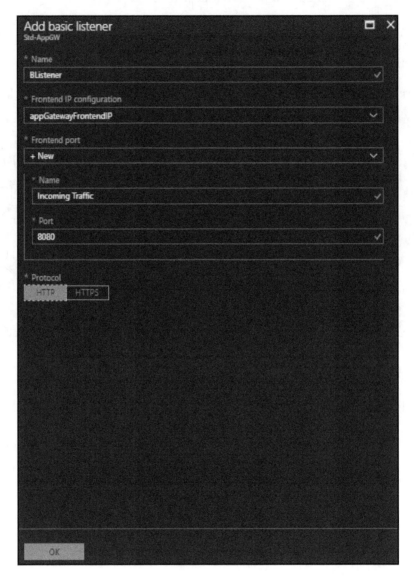

Figure 8.19: Creating a basic listener

4. Once you have clicked on **OK**, the listener will be added within a moment.

 If you create a frontend port, you can reuse it with other listeners.

Configuring multi-site listener

To configure the multi-site listener, you need to follow these steps:

1. Navigate to the application gateway
2. Under **SETTINGS**, click on **Listeners**, and a new blade will be opened
3. Click on **Multi-site** and a new blade will be opened wherein you have to specify the following:
   - **Name**: Specify a descriptive name for the listener
   - **Frontend IP configuration**: Select the frontend IP configurations that should be associated with the listener
   - **Frontend port**: You can either select a pre-created frontend port or create a new one
   - **Host name**: Specify the host name on which multiple websites are hosted

- **Protocol**: Specify the used protocol whether it is **HTTP** or **HTTPS**

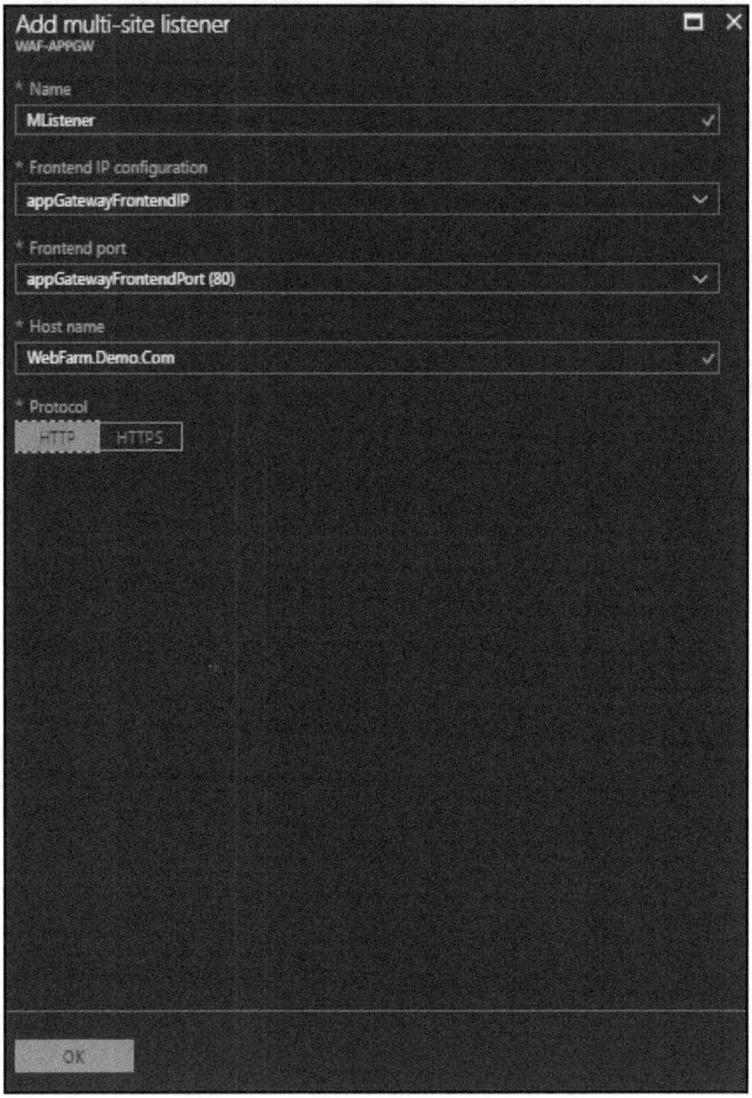

Figure 8.20: Create multi-site listener

4. Once you have clicked on **OK**, the listener will be added

Configuring rules

Rules are used to specify how the traffic will flow. The following are two types of rules:

- **Basic**: In this case, any incoming traffic might access the desired content from multiple backend servers
- **Path-based**: In this case, if you want to access a specific content, you will access specific backend servers to access the content

Configuring basic rule

To configure a basic rule, you need to follow these steps:

1. Navigate to the application gateway
2. Under **SETTINGS**, click on **Rules**, and a new blade will be opened, as shown in the following screenshot:

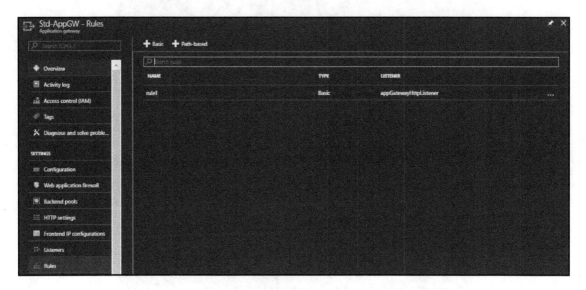

Figure 8.21: Application gateway rules

3. To add a basic rule, click on **Basic**, and a new blade will be opened wherein you have to specify the following:
   - **Name**: Specify a descriptive name for the rule
   - **Listener**: Specify the listener to which this rule will be associated

- **Backend pool**: Specify the backend pool to which this rule will be associated
- **HTTP setting**: Specify to which HTTP setting this rule will be associated

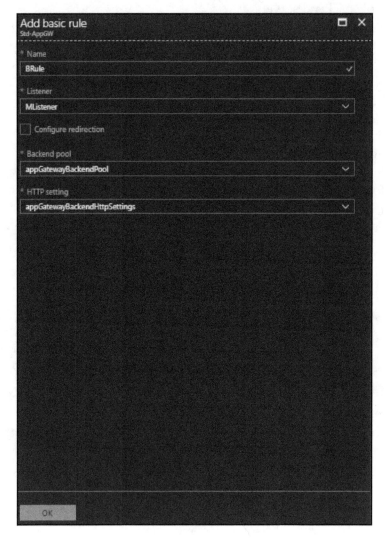

Figure 8.22: Configure basic rule

4. Once you are done, click on **OK** and the rule will be created.

Configuring path-based rule

To configure a path-based rule, you need to follow these steps:

1. Navigate to the application gateway
2. Under **SETTINGS**, click on **Rules**, and a new blade will be opened
3. To add a path-based rule, click on **Path-based**, and a new blade will be opened wherein you have to specify the following:
    - **Name**: Specify a descriptive name for the rule
    - **Listener**: Specify the listener that will be associated with this rule
    - **Default backend pool**: Specify the backend pool to which this rule will be associated
    - **Default HTTP settings**: Specify the HTTP settings that will be associated with this rule
4. Then, you have to specify the paths by specifying the following:
    - **NAME**: Specify a descriptive name for the path
    - **PATHS**: Specify the path itself
    - **BACKEND POOL**: Specify the backend pool on which this path exists

- **HTTP SETTINGS**: Specify the HTTP settings that will be applied

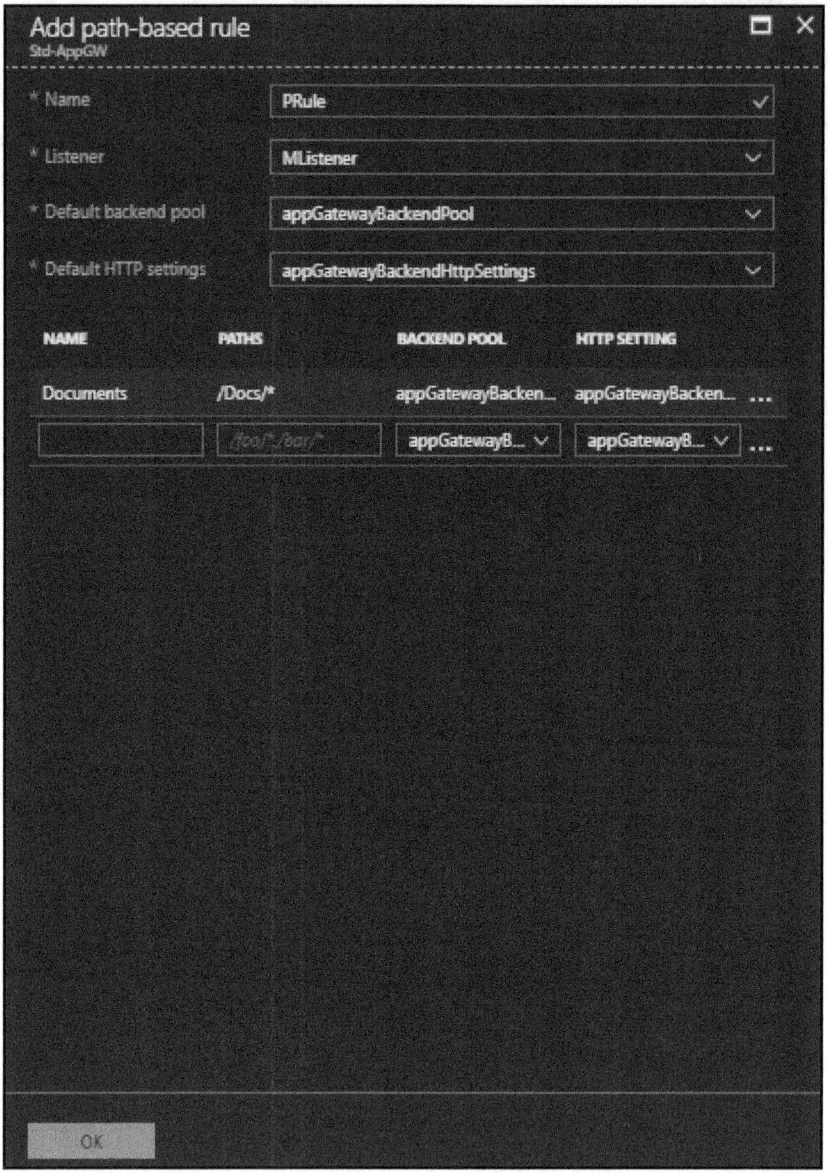

Figure 8.23: Configure path-based rule

5. Once you are done, click on **OK**, and the rule will be added

Configuring health probes

By now, you should be aware that probes are used to monitor the health of the backend pool. You can create and customize probes according to your needs. To do so, you need to follow these steps:

1. Navigate to the application gateway.
2. Under **SETTINGS**, click on **Health probes**, and a new blade will be opened:

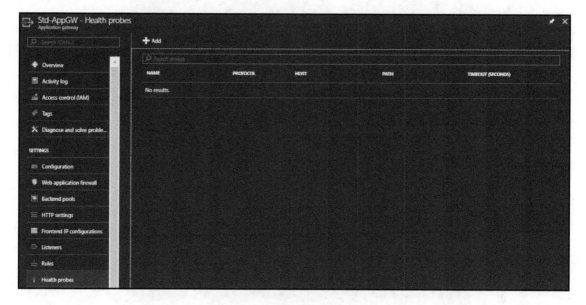

Figure 8.24: Health probes

3. To create health probes, click on **Add**, and a new blade will be opened wherein you have to specify the following:
   - **Name**: A descriptive name for the health probe
   - **Protocol**: Select the protocol you use, whether it is HTTP or HTTPS
   - **Host**: Specify the host that you want to monitor
   - **Path**: Specify which path you want to monitor
   - **Interval (seconds)**: The period after which a new probe is being sent
   - **Timeout (seconds)**: The period after which the probe will be considered unresponsive

- **Unhealthy threshold**: The number of unresponsive probes after which the host will be considered unhealthy

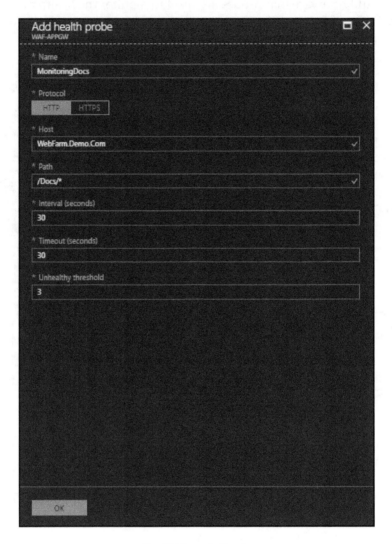

Figure 8.25: Create a health probe

4. Once you are done, you can click on **OK**, and the health probe will be created.

Summary

It was a fruitful journey working with Azure networking solutions. More importantly, you should have learned by now how to work with most of the networking solutions supported on Azure. Also, with the knowledge gained throughout the chapters, you should be able to design a solution that would suit your environment. We hope you have gained the knowledge you need from this book, and we hope you enjoyed reading it as much as I enjoyed writing it.

Questions

- Azure Application Gateway provides a layer 7 load balancing for any type of traffic (true/false)
- You can upgrade a standard Application Gateway to WAF (true/false)
- You can configure rules for the Application Gateway based on the content path (true/false)
- State and explain three of the Azure Application Gateway features
- State the types of Azure Application Gateway and the sizes of them
- State and explain the types of Azure Application Gateway listeners
- What is the maximum number of instances per Azure Application Gateway?

Further reading

If you are interested to know more about the topics that have been covered, you can check the following links:

- **Creating an application gateway and virtual machine scale set using Azure PowerShell**: https://docs.microsoft.com/en-us/azure/application-gateway/tutorial-create-vmss-powershell
- **Application Gateway redirect overview**: https://docs.microsoft.com/en-us/azure/application-gateway/application-gateway-redirect-overview

- **Configuring App Service Web Apps with Application Gateway**: `https://docs.microsoft.com/en-us/azure/application-gateway/application-gateway-web-app-powershell`
- **Using load balancing services in Azure**: `https://docs.microsoft.com/en-us/azure/traffic-manager/traffic-manager-load-balancing-azure?toc=%2fazure%2fapplication-gateway%2ftoc.json`

Other Books You May Enjoy

If you enjoyed this book, you may be interested in these other books by Packt:

Azure for Architects
Ritesh Modi

ISBN: 978-1-78839-739-1

- Familiarize yourself with the components of the Azure Cloud platform
- Understand the cloud design patterns
- Use enterprise security guidelines for your Azure deployment
- Design and implement Serverless solutions
- See Cloud architecture and the deployment pipeline
- Understand cost management for Azure solutions

Azure Serverless Computing Cookbook

Praveen Kumar Sreeram

ISBN: 978-1-78839-082-8

- Develop different event-based handlers supported by serverless architecture supported by Microsoft Cloud Platform – Azure
- Integrate Azure Functions with different Azure Services to develop Enterprise-level applications
- Get to know the best practices in organizing and refactoring the code within the Azure functions
- Test, troubleshoot, and monitor the Azure functions to deliver high-quality, reliable, and robust cloud-centric applications
- Automate mundane tasks at various levels right from development to deployment and maintenance
- Learn how to develop stateful serverless applications and also self-healing jobs using Durable Functions

Leave a review - let other readers know what you think

Please share your thoughts on this book with others by leaving a review on the site that you bought it from. If you purchased the book from Amazon, please leave us an honest review on this book's Amazon page. This is vital so that other potential readers can see and use your unbiased opinion to make purchasing decisions, we can understand what our customers think about our products, and our authors can see your feedback on the title that they have worked with Packt to create. It will only take a few minutes of your time, but is valuable to other potential customers, our authors, and Packt. Thank you!

Index

www.ingramcontent.com/pod-product-compliance
Lightning Source LLC
LaVergne TN
LVHW081520050326
832903LV00025B/1555